POOR KIT SMART

Poor Kit Smart

CHRISTOPHER DEVLIN

Southern Illinois University Press

CARBONDALE

Printed in Great Britain by
Western Printing Services Limited, Bristol

to

CLARE *and* JULIAN

with love

Acknowledgments

THE way in which this book came to be written required a great deal of help from friends both old and new—so much that to record it all would be quite out of proportion to the book's modest size and scope. I must, however, express my gratitude to the following. To Archbishop King for a copy of the Cowslade MS dealing with Smart's wife and daughters. To Lord Barnard for kind permission to use his family papers and assistance in using them. To Mrs Edington and to Mrs Stokes for locating and transcribing some very long documents. To Mr J. A. Woods for the reference to Smart in the Sharp letters, which I did not know of, and to Miss Lloyd-Baker, owner of the letters. To Dr Richard Hunter for sending me extracts from the Committee Book of St Luke's. To Mr Stanley Horrocks, head of the Reading public library, who introduced me to the very extensive collection of Smartiana that is kept there.

The quotations from *Jubilate Agno* follow the text established by Mr W. H. Bond in 1954, and those from all the other poems *The Collected Poems* edited by Norman Callan in 1949.

C. D.

Contents

1 Who was Christopher Smart?   9
2 Boyhood   23
3 Cambridge   36
4 London   48
5 Marriage   62
6 Madness   76
7 At St Luke's Asylum   88
8 *Jubilate Agno*   101
9 "At Chelsey or Elsewhere"   116
10 Release   128
11 The Immortal Song   138
12 Strains and Quarrels   152
13 Failure and Isolation   167
14 "We never are deserted quite"   182

ONE

❖

Who was Christopher Smart?

THERE are three Christopher Smarts. The coffee-house genius of eighteenth-century London who knew everyone that was worth knowing. The solitary ghost who visited poets of the nineteenth century, sang one song of surpassing grandeur, then vanished into the mist again. And finally the Christopher Smart whom critics of the twentieth century are still trying to discover and reconstruct.

The Christopher Smart whom his London friends preferred to remember, before the tragedy that broke his life, was a spruce and jolly little man with immaculate cravat and ruffles. He twinkled with a quick hesitating charm, and he sparkled with a succession of qualities that picked him out like a star from the dull mass of Grub Street where he had chosen to earn his living.

To begin with, he had the lustre of scholarship. A Fellow of Pembroke and Praelector in Philosophy and Rhetoric, his college had clung to him, in spite of his bad behaviour, long after the year 1749 when he had deserted Cambridge University for London Town. That was because he was a successful poet; with the greatest of ease he won for his college the Seatonian Prize Poem five times between 1750 and 1755—that is, every time he entered for it.

To win fame as a poet in those barren years after the death of Pope was rare. There was no doubt that Smart had the gift, the *curiosa felicitas*, the happy inventiveness that sealed him as a genuine "Bard", and he carried also, like a twinkling decoration on his chest, the compliments which Mr. Pope himself before his death had taken the trouble to pay him. You might say that Thomas Gray was a better poet than Smart and more of a credit to Cambridge. But Gray was a difficult man and his poetry came with difficulty. Smart just "lisped in numbers and the numbers came"; he could write about anything, serious or comic, with the same dash and gusto.

Besides the gift of poetry he had something else, most necessary for success in literary London; he had the gift of conversation. Wherever he went there was laughter, with him, or against him, he did not mind which, so long as it was happy and spontaneous. Men who were his seniors, whose names are now immortal—Johnson, Hogarth, Garrick, Fielding and Smollett—were glad to call him friend; so were the younger generation: Goldsmith, Churchill and Cowper. Scholar, poet, wit, it was perhaps as a wit that he was best known to his contemporaries, and it is a pity that Boswell was ten years too late to record his sayings.

Scholar, poet, wit, Smart was also a gentleman—with a coat of arms and a not undistinguished pedigree. But this was the part that he played least successfully. He was not a snob, he valued virtue and talent higher than birth, but he was too helplessly "all things to all men." With a hankering both for low company and for high society, he simply had not the means to keep up with the various sprigs of nobility who were pleased to know him. From these attempts to play the gentleman came his two most obvious weaknesses, tippling and extravagance; he drank like a lord and he threw his money about with a lordly generosity. They were common enough weaknesses at the time, and they were not rooted in Smart but only occasional; he would probably have outgrown them in the normal way.

But he had a third weakness, at first a tiny cloud no bigger than a man's hand; it took all his friends and relatives completely by surprise when it suddenly burst with the violence of a storm. But I think Thomas Gray of all people had noticed it several years before at Cambridge. Gray was Smart's senior by six years. He had for his young colleague a kind of exasperated affection which masked itself as pity but which in fact concealed a certain envy. I do not think this envy was due to Smart's far greater facility in verse, for Gray and his friends could genuinely afford to despise the dreary imitations of Pope which they had determined to strike away from. The envy, I think, was because he divined in Smart a familiarity with a spring of inspiration which he himself could approach only with great caution and diffidence.

Gray and his friend Thomas Warton at Cambridge, like William Collins and Joseph Warton at Oxford, had caught the infection of *wild nature*. I mean the challenge, which the elder poet, James Thomson, had initiated, to communicate the presence of *something* that eluded the ordinary powers of sense and reason. In the years between 1746 and 1749 Collins, with Thomson's encouragement, had written his matchless Odes. In 1750 Gray had written his immortal Elegy. In the same year Collins had become permanently insane.

At that time—the time of the great preachings of Wesley and Whitfield—the chief cause of insanity was reckoned to be religious mania. "Of that," said the Lord Chancellor of the day severely, "not only Bedlam but most of the private mad-houses are melancholy and striking proofs." At the same time it was an ancient truism that religious mania and poetic inspiration were closely connected. Was it not for that very reason that Plato had banished poets from his Republic? As the Greeks of the classical age abhorred the frenzies of Dionysus, so did all sound men of the eighteenth century maintain stout barriers against "enthusiasm"—by which they meant any unauthorized overstepping of the natural bounds of reason.

Gray was very conscious of the danger of madness coming from "enthusiasm" whether religious or poetic. He was a nervous, irritable, melancholy man. The difficulty of what he was trying to do (I mean, to express wild nature) and the terrible fate of Collins weighed upon his mind. In his *Elegy* he had written:

> The ploughman homeward plods his weary way
> And leaves the world to darkness and to me.

"And to me"? At least there should have been that consolation: that he was the lonely pioneer and proprietor of this new, untamed territory. But here was this young Smart who,

11

when he wanted, could whistle like a ploughboy strolling out of the wild wood and could make the birds whistle with him. In the midst of the staid blank-verse effusions which won the Prize Poem for Smart year after year there would be, time and again, naive outbursts like the following in 1751:

> Yet Thou art there, yet God himself is there
> Ev'n on the bush (tho' not as when to Moses
> He shone in burning Majesty reveal'd)
> Nathless conspicuous in the linnet's throat
> Is his unbounded goodness—Thee her Maker,
> Thee her Preserver chants she in her song;

or this in 1756:

> And lo! they call; the blackbird and the thrush,
> The woodlark, and the redbreast jointly call;
> He hears and feeds their feather'd families,
> He feeds his sweet musicians—nor neglects
> The invoking ravens in the greenwood wide;
> And though their throats coarse ruttling hurt the ear,
> They mean it all for music, thanks and praise
> They mean, and leave ingratitude to man,—

It was most unusual for a poet in those days to know the names of more than half a dozen typical birds. Smart not only knew the names and habits of innumerable birds, beasts, fishes and insects, but he seemed to feel a strange kinship with them. To Gray there was something very alarming about Smart's sense of intimate communion with all created beings, about the tremor of "enthusiasm" which occasionally ran through his light-hearted verse.

But nobody else, so far as I know, had the least suspicion of Smart's sanity. It came as an utter shock to friends and relatives when this polished little man-about-town was struck and riven by that most dreaded and ludicrous of all diseases—religious mania. It opened like a trap-door beneath his feet and he disappeared completely. His friends averted their eyes and preferred to remember him as he had been before this fate destroyed him.

That last statement is not accurate as an immediate chronicle of events; several friends made gallant and persevering efforts to save him. But in the end they averted their eyes. The statement is true about the general effect.

Smart spent seven years in confinement, public or private, and eight more years after that before his death in 1771, and during those last fifteen years he produced a large mass of verse and managed to get most of it published. Yet, apart from a few embarrassed half-compliments, this mass of work never had any recognition among his former admirers, whilst among his former enemies it produced derisive sniggers. "It would be cruel to criticize," lisped the *Monthly Review* about a piece called *A Song to David*, since apparently

> it was written when the Author was denied the use of pen, ink and paper, and was obliged to indent his lines with the end of a key upon the wainscot.

Others contented themselves with veiled pitying allusions to his breakdown and confinement—"melancholy occasion," "unhappy circumstances," "this unfortunate gentleman," "a fine piece of ruins," "his departed muse."

Consequently, when Smart's relatives twenty years after his death published his *Poems* in two volumes, they practically confined them to those written before his breakdown in 1756. The volumes were edited by Smart's nephew, Christopher Hunter, and printed by Smart's widow who was then proprietor and editor of the *Reading Mercury*. (Mrs Smart's father, William Carnan, was one of the founders of this fine provincial newspaper.) Hunter in his memoir made euphemistic references to his uncle's "melancholy disorders," but gave no indication that any other poetry had been produced during that period—except that at the end of the memoir there is an asterisk, and under the asterisk a footnote or postscript:

> Besides the works contained in this edition, our Author wrote a Poem called a *Song to David*, and a new *Version of the Psalms*: he also translated the Works of Horace, and the Fables of Phaedrus into English Metre; and versified our Saviour's Parables. These with two small pamphlets of Poems, were written after his confinement, and bear for the most part melancholy proofs of the recent estrangement of his mind. Such poems however have been selected from his pamphlets and inserted in the present work, as were likely to be acceptable to the Reader.

Thus was the line firmly drawn in that century. An anthology of religious verse published in 1800 gives generous space to Smart, but all the extracts are from his Cambridge prize poems, written before 1756.

The nineteenth-century view of Smart was entirely different. Yet it took its rise directly from the eighteenth. Its origin was that ridiculous legend circulated by the *Monthly Review* in 1763 that Smart wrote his *Song to David* on the madhouse wall, being denied the use of pen, ink and paper.

Already his daughter, Mrs Smart Le Noir, had in print in 1826 rebuked this invention as "too absurd for refutation." But the story was too attractive to be resisted by the Romantics.

Poets in the high summer of the nineteenth century gazed back at the Age of Reason across a great gulf made by the French Revolution, the Industrial Revolution, the Romantic Movement and the various reform bills. For the most part they saw its poetry as a lumber-room of dusty junk, or, rather, as a leafless, winter-sodden landscape which had since been utterly transformed by the spring and early summer of Wordsworth and Coleridge, Keats and Shelley. Yet occasionally in those barren wastes they discerned a few gleams of untimely loveliness, frail prophets of the glory to come. Among these forerunners it was notable how many had succumbed to the suffocating pressure of the Age of Reason. William Collins had been shut up for life at the age of thirty. Chatterton, the boy-wonder mourned by Keats and Shelley, had killed himself before he was twenty. And now a third tragic face joined them: that of Christopher Smart, twisted into a pathetic frenzy behind the bars of his cage, his trembling hands trying to inscribe the frantic message of his verse upon the madhouse wall.

The frantic message was entitled *A Song to David*; it turned out to be an astoundingly beautiful, perfectly finished poem, over 500 lines in length, which Smart himself had caused to be published in 1763. Its re-publication in the nineteenth century caught the attention of the great Victorians. Wordsworth had copied out several stanzas but had made no public comment. Robert Browning, however, D. G. Rossetti and Sir Francis Palgrave proclaimed aloud that this madman's

Song to David was among the masterpieces of the English language.

Browning himself wrote a long poem about David which was obviously suggested by Smart's *Song*, and he wrote also a fair chunk of inferior verse describing the effect of the *Song* upon him. It was like having walked through a huge house, he said, room after room in dull and decent order, and then suddenly opening a door upon the Chapel—a blinding glow of religious inspiration in coloured glass and sculpted symmetry. Even so, he repeated, was the *Song to David*, unique in the century and in Smart's life, and highest poetic point between Milton and Keats:

> out of throngs between
> Milton and Keats, who donned the singing-dress,
> Smart, solely of such songmen, pierced the screen
> Twixt thing and word, lit language straight from soul

"Pierced the screen twixt thing and word" is a vivid way of putting what several more recent critics have said about Smart's accomplishment in the *Song to David*.

This however was not the general opinion of the century. In general Smart was quite unknown among those to whom Gray's *Elegy* was a household word. Those who had occasion to come across his name knew him only vaguely as "a sot and a wastrel" visited by one brief fit of doubtful inspiration which he had inscribed upon a madhouse wall. The authors of *The Church in the Eighteenth Century*, two learned and interesting volumes published by Longmans in 1878, have a long chapter on sacred poetry in which Smart claims a few lines; the "key upon the wainscot" story of the *Song's* origin is repeated, and the authors conclude:

> No copy of the poem is now, as it appears, known to be extant, but a few stanzas, remarkable for their animation, have been preserved.

The gentle unconscious irony of this will be more appreciated when it is realized that the entirety of Smart's last fifteen years with its huge literary output was intended directly for the adornment of the Church of England.

Smart, then, in the nineteenth century was a "poet's poet." The very few who admired him, admired him intensely, but even to them he was a bodiless figure, a face floating in the mist, from whose pallid lips came forth one *Song* of matchless beauty. This spiritual approach of the poet to the poet has been described in haunting words by Dame Edith Sitwell writing in 1930:

> But the whole poem is bathed in the everlasting light of Heaven; the flowers are brighter than they are in our earthly meadows; there is no room in the heaven of this madman's mind for cruelty or injustice, or for anything but love. That Heaven was undimmed by the cruelties and by the darkness of Bedlam, unbroken by starvation, warm in the midst of that deathly cold. This madman of genius, this poet of genius, for all the barriers of his madness, continued to walk in the cool of the evening with his God.

But already in the twentieth century, with the second centenary of Smart's birth (1722), a new attitude was being adopted. There was the beginning of an attempt to adjust the forlorn, romantic nineteenth-century head to the tubby little eighteenth-century body and to make some sense of the result.

A glance at the bibliography on page 194 will show the sudden spurt of interest in Christopher Smart around 1923 and 1924.

The *Reading Mercury* published a Bicentenary Supplement in 1923 with an account of Smart's sturdy descendants who governed this newspaper for a hundred and fifty years (1762–1914). It also reproduced for the first time the portrait of Christopher Smart, head and body complete, which was then the property of his descendants.

In 1924 three books about Smart were published, all of which had this novelty about them: taking for granted the excellence of *A Song to David*, they explored the *rest* of the poetry that Smart wrote after his confinement. I will note here only one or two points in them that have helped to suggest the present study.

Edmund Blunden, the poet, writing with the cool detachment of a critic, observed "a main innocence, a fine sensibility" that ran through the whole of Smart's life; he also noted the importance of a longish poem written in 1756, the year that was the bridge between the old life and the new.

Middleton Murry, a critic writing with the fervour of a

16

poet, could find only one adjective to express properly the savour of Smart's short religious lyrics and indeed to describe Smart's whole attitude—"Franciscan." The adjective Franciscan is sometimes used in a way that has no relation to the actual life history of St Francis of Assisi. But in this case there is at least a *prima facie* resemblance—poverty, humiliation and suffering accepted without rancour and even with a kind of joy.

After 1924, apart from shorter notices and articles, there was a dearth of *Smartiana* until suddenly in 1939 came the publication of a most exciting discovery. Mr W. F. Stead discovered thirty-two pages in Smart's own hand of a composition entitled *Jubilate Agno* ("Rejoice in the Lamb") written while he was in confinement as a lunatic. It was written in a sort of free verse, most of the verses beginning with the word "Let" and the remainder with the word "For." The general purpose of the "Let" verses was to summon different personages, Biblical at first and then non-Biblical, to bless God—each in conjunction with some individual of the animal or plant world, so that the total effect would be a chorus of praise from all creation. But after several hundred lines the purpose appears to degenerate into a meaningless list of oddities, while the "For" verses do not seem to make even the beginning of a coherent plan.

In later chapters of this study there will be a great deal more to say about *Jubilate Agno*. Here I am concerned only with the immediate effect of Mr Stead's edition upon the twentieth-century reconstruction of Smart. Mr Stead is as certain that *Jubilate Agno* is a "melancholy proof of the recent estrangement of his mind" as was the Rev Christopher Hunter about *A Song to David*. But he is much less certain than Hunter about the genuineness of Smart's piety:

> The trouble with Smart's religion was that he mingled his prayers with strong drink; he prayed, and got drunk; he prayed again, and then he got drunk again, exhibiting such a chaotic discontinuity of thought as is only too conspicuous in this manuscript.

On the other hand the manuscript arouses in him a pitying affection for the childlike pathos of Smart's attitude, so that his final comment has a certain ambivalence:

> The value of the manuscript as a whole . . . is twofold; it throws a flood of light upon the sources of *A Song to David*, and it tells us a great deal about Smart which can be found nowhere else. The more I see of Smart, the more I like him. I know that he never abandoned his follies; to the end of his days he indulged in periods of "bacchanalian forgetfulness"; he was never able to live according to any principle; he developed no character, he ruined his mind. Yet there were qualities in the man which more than balanced his faults; a childlike innocence, a bright celestial vision, a heart which was always affectionate, and a faith which survived years of misery and humiliation.

The year of the publication of this manuscript, 1939, was also the year of the outbreak of the Second World War. The manuscript went to America, to the Harvard University Library. The next important study of Smart came in 1943 conjointly from two American scholars, Professors Edward G. Ainsworth and Charles E. Noyes of the University of Missouri, Columbia. This study is of immense value in collating and documenting all the available information about Smart. But here, as I have said, I am concerned only with its contribution towards a coherent character of Smart.

The authors are at pains to show the continuity between the two halves of his life, before and after 1756. They find the chief element in this continuity to be the "ruinous weakness" of Smart's will. They underline three tragic crises when this weakness ruined him, first when he threw up his prospects at Cambridge, secondly when he gave up all effort to support his family in London and lapsed into insanity, and finally when, after a reformation of morals in the madhouse, he slipped again and ended his days as a drunkard in the debtors' gaol. "Others always helped Smart, but he could not or would not help himself."

They take it for granted that by 1756 he was a confirmed inebriate and a public nuisance, and even their tributes to his friendly nature are tempered by such severe comments as the following: "There was nothing offensive in the man save his devil's vanity and his egotistic self-pity." In their account the elements in Smart's insanity are very clearly implied: alcoholism, delusions of grandeur and persecution-mania.

These elements were more explicitly described in 1949 by

Mr Norman Callan in his Muses Library two-volume edition of the *Collected Poems of Christopher Smart*. Mr Callan gives a very brilliant and subtle appreciation of Smart's poetry; but it is at the expense of Smart's character:

> Like Donne and Milton, he is persistently egocentric, but whereas they show the ego at grips with the great problems of humanity, Smart's ego seems too often entangled in a pettifogging exhibitionism. His tone is so personal that unless the reader is prepared to make the effort to understand his personality he is continually subject to a feeling of irritation at the self-absorption everywhere apparent.

Elsewhere in the introduction Mr Callan has said of Smart, "The temptation to take sides . . . is to be resisted"; but it is not clear whether he has overcome his "irritation" and is making a considered judgment when he continues:

> He is one of those people who never outgrows the inferiorities and assertiveness of childhood. He oscillates between extremes of self-belittlement and self-glorification, between
>
> *For I am a little fellow . . .*
>
> and
>
> . . . now the deed's
> DETERMINED, DARED and DONE.

This is a reference to the last lines of *A Song to David*:

> And now the matchless deed's atchiev'd,
> DETERMINED, DARED, and DONE.

Mr Callan's irritation seems to have led him astray here; for Smart was talking quite patently, not about his own achievement, but about the Incarnation foreshadowed by David. Moreover, one has only to read him to see that he did not in the least mind being "a little fellow"; all his allusions to his small size are made with a good-humoured chuckle.

A slip like this on the part of so competent a critic makes one query retrospectively the gloomy headshaking of Mr Stead and Professors Ainsworth and Noyes about Smart's character: how much of the gloom depends upon evidence and how much on irritation?

But even at the moment when Smart was being catalogued as an unprincipled neurotic, a trumpet was sounding for him on the other side of the Atlantic. In 1950 a selected edition of his poetry by Mr Robert Brittain of Princeton University contained a 70-page introduction with by far the fullest and most rounded *and* most sympathetic portrait of Smart that had yet appeared. It was especially welcome, after the *de haut en bas* tone of previous critics, to find Smart treated as an adult instead of a delinquent child. As Mr Brittain says:

> The blemishes in his work, like those in his character, are obvious even to the undiscerning. Yet his admirers need offer no apologies for him, for his genuine virtues should be as obvious as his faults.

It must be admitted, however, that Smart is made to shine at the expense, particularly, of John Newbery, his publisher, and Anna-Maria Carnan, his wife, who are handled very sharply. The picture one gets is of a gentle, over-sensitive genius hounded into a breakdown by callous and pettifogging philistines. But here again a little slip makes one wonder: "It is interesting that Smart never talks of catching fish: he always seems content to watch them and let them be," writes Mr Brittain to illustrate the poet's sweetness of nature. But what about: "it is good to angle with meditation," the list from Izaak Walton, and "Mr FLETCHER who has my tackling"? No, Smart was a fisherman all right. And he had a strain of toughness ("tykishness" you might call it) which I do not think Mr Brittain allows for. Nevertheless his is the first study, since Mr Edmund Blunden's very short account, in which one feels one is getting to grips with a man and not a nebulous projection.

With the publication of Mr Brittain's book the tide of comment seems to have changed definitely in favour of Smart's character. The next development in his reconstruction was of the greatest importance.

It occurred in 1954. Mr W. H. Bond, Curator of Manuscripts at the Harvard Library, discovered that the thirty-two pages of *Jubilate Agno* had never yet been printed in the right order. To be brief, the "For" verses should have been printed alongside of the "Let" verses, like the antiphons of Hebraic poetry which Smart was obviously imitating. Mr Bond's conclusive proof of this in his 1954 edition did not in any way diminish the value of Mr Stead's learned notes to the 1939 edition, but it did shed a completely new light on the composition of *Jubilate Agno*.

It showed first that Smart began his poem with a coherent plan and a fine sweep of execution; but so many of the early pages are missing that it is impossible to judge it as a finished work; one can only say that it is much less lunatic than was at first supposed. Secondly, it is clear that long before the end Smart had abandoned any idea of having the work published; he continued it, at the rate of one verse a day, simply as a means of marking off the dates until the time appointed for his release. To write a paragraph of learned nonsense once a day may not, after all, be an indication of insanity so much as a method of *keeping sane* in difficult circumstances.

On the question of the sanity of the poem Mr Bond comments that "research has provided authorities for many of the wildest of Smart's flights, with the result that the burden of proof now rests with those who would claim that a given passage represents pure fancy or the ravings of a madman." And concerning Smart's character: "The sweetness of spirit which distinguishes much of this work becomes the more astonishing when viewed against the background of bitter circumstance which closed in upon him."

More recent researches on *Jubilate Agno* have confirmed, in the words of Professor Sherbo of Michigan, "much greater sanity and order—and ingenious method—in the poem than has been suspected hitherto."

Non-recognition of this and of the 1954 edition of *Jubilate Agno* rather weaken a recent verdict on Smart by the distinguished neurologist Sir Russell Brain—that Smart was a cyclothyme, subject to alternating fits of exaltation and depression. I mean that it leaves the extent of his cyclothymia still in doubt—I suppose a lot of people are cycloid up to a point; Sir Russell applies the term to many literary men, including Boswell and Johnson, who were not lunatics. Moreover, though cyclothymia may be a correct medical label for Smart, it does not throw any light on his character nor on the particular obsession that was his real trouble.

So far, then, the critics of the last twenty or thirty years have failed to produce a coherent character for Christopher Smart. What was emerging up to 1950 was a confirmed inebriate with unpleasant habits and no principles; but after 1950 the lineaments are those of a high-minded, long-suffering, misunderstood genius. There is room, I think, for an attempt to fuse the two into some sort of verisimilitude of a man.

Moreover there are aspects and details of Smart's life that have hardly been touched as yet by biographers. Religion was the main force that dominated him; yet hardly any attempt has been made to analyse his ideas and impulses, mystical or maniacal or whatever they were. Closely allied to his religion was his marriage and the shipwreck that came of it; no writer on Smart seems aware that his wife was a devout Roman Catholic when he married her.[1]

There are certain facts, also, that have not been hitherto mentioned. One, for example, is his expectation of inheriting the ancestral manor on Staindrop Moor. Another is the evidence for the place of his second confinement.

Finally there is the question of madness and his masterpiece. Was it his mania that made possible his solitary masterpiece, *A Song to David*? Or was it rather, as I think, obsessive mania that *prevented* him from ever writing anything else so good?

Far more research is needed on these half-discovered points than has been possible for a book of this size and scope. But, even so, there is enough to give new impulse and interest to a re-telling of the tale, especially since it has to steer its course between opposing sides.

[1] Mr Brittain alone mentions her religion, but thinks, wrongly, that she was a convert in later life.

TWO

Boyhood

CHRISTOPHER came of a Durham family that claimed the ancestry and blazon of Sir John Smart, Garter King-at-Arms under Edward IV. The most notable forebear was Dr Peter Smart, prebendary of Durham Cathedral and head-master of the Grammar School, whose violent Puritanism made him a thorn in the side of the Established Church for nearly fifty years. He spent ten of them in the King's Bench Prison, but triumphed in the end with the downfall of Laud and Charles I. It was probably this Peter who in 1629 bequeathed an estate called Snotterton in the parish of Stain-drop to John Smart and his heirs to hold for ever—some time before the famous Parliamentary family of the Vanes acquired Raby Castle nearby, the former seat of the Nevilles. John's grandson Francis (1653–1716), who inherited Snotterton, was Christopher's grandfather; he married Margaret Gilpin, who was descended from a well-known preacher, Bernard Gilpin, called "The Apostle of the North." Christopher thus had a double legacy of religious enthusiasm, and was well aware of it, for he was very proud of his ancestors.

Francis had two sons, John, who inherited Snotterton, and Peter (1687–1733), who married Winifred Griffiths, a Welsh-woman from Radnor. This Peter, Christopher's father, was destined for the Church but instead became steward to the Kentish estates of Christopher Vane, first Lord Barnard, who probably gave his name to Peter's son.

So it came about that Christopher and his two sisters, Marianne and Margaret, were all born in Kent—at Shipbourne

...in the middle of the hop country. Marianne was born 11 October 1720, Christopher 11 April 1722, Margaret some time earlier. The earliest reminiscence of Christopher comes from "his eldest sister Margaret"[1] who says that at the age of four he wrote a love-poem to a girl three times his age which contained these appealing lines:

> Madam if you please to pity
> O poor Kitty, O poor Kitty.

Hunter (Margaret's son) comments on his uncle's sickly infancy and the early use of "cordials" which, he surmises, may have been responsible for later deviations from sobriety. It sounds an old wives' tale, but Smart may have remembered it, long after, as a grievance against his family. Later biographers are more interested in the preponderant feminine influence in his early life, which they find "significant"; but significant of *what* is not stated. There was nothing particularly effeminate about Smart at any known period of his life. He was, however, a boyish "platonist"; he reached up towards and personified to himself, as many boys do, a semi-divine female figure, "the daughter of God," whom in youth he called "Good Nature" or "his muse," and in later life "Charity" or "Gratitude."

The fairest impression of Smart's Kentish childhood is that it was uninhibitedly happy:

> 'Twas Mercury that rul'd my natal morn,
> What time the Sun exerts his genial ray,
> And ripens for enjoyment every growing day;
> When to exist is but to love and sing,
> And sprightly Aries smiles upon the spring.

He had nothing but delightful recollections of that soft and fruitful countryside through which the Medway flows. The visual memories are preserved in *The Hop-Garden* and *A Noon-Piece*—bad poems with a few good lines. All the good lines are those about the silver Medway, the different fish that glide beneath its waters, the magical reflections of trees and distant towers. Its banks became in his mind not only a storehouse of imagery, but a sort of cushion of happiness on which he could recline in times of adversity.

[1] In the letter of Smart's daughter Elizabeth; see Bibliography.

Peter Smart, his father, was a widely-read man (Hunter informs us) and Christopher from an early age had the benefit of a well-stocked library. One would like to know if its shelves contained the Elizabethan and Caroline poets; for these, especially Andrew Marvell, seem to have been Christopher's most beneficent models. He was a verse-maker from a very early age; but his father did not live to see the seeds he had planted springing into full growth. He died untimely in 1733. Christopher, a schoolboy at Maidstone, was then aged eleven.

On the death of Peter Smart his widow left Kent with her children and returned to Durham. This was done especially for Christopher's benefit, so that he should have—says Hunter—"the advantages of a good school, change of air to strengthen a weakly frame, and the notice and protection of his Father's relations." As to his father's relations, they were at that time his uncle, John Smart of Snotterton, and John's son, Francis. But there is no record that any help was ever forthcoming from them; rather the reverse.

Winifred Smart at that time had to manage on very little, and Christopher would have had no worldly prospects, if it had not been for the kindness of the Vane family. Winifred Smart was a Welsh woman, as has been said, and her Welshness was something which her son, for some reason, always remembered with pride and affection. "For I am the seed of the WELCH WOMAN," he wrote later, "and speak the truth from my heart." Perhaps it was from her he got his fondness for genealogies and for the Romano-Celtic legends of this island. What he certainly got from her was effective encouragement to work hard at his books.

He was taken in at Durham Grammar School where his surname was so well known and honoured and where the headmaster, the Reverend Richard Dongworth, an old Etonian, was a fine teacher. Christopher, an industrious and successful pupil, received a grounding in Latin and Greek which proved decisive for his future career at Cambridge.

Equally decisive was the kindly patronage of the elder branch of the Vanes represented by Lord Barnard of Raby Castle, who remembered the services of Peter Smart to the family. The children were often invited to come and spend their holidays at the castle. Lord Barnard had a boy and a girl of about the same age as Christopher and his sisters, Margaret and Marianne. Christopher's bright nature and happy cleverness made such a favourable impression that Lord Barnard's mother-in-law, the Duchess of Cleveland, promised to see him through his University career with the handsome sum of £40 a year.

It was during one of these holidays at Raby that an incident occurred which has fascinated all Smart's recent biographers looking for an early flaw in his composition. The only authority for it is the prattling letter of reminiscence by Mrs Le Noir, Smart's younger daughter, whose source was obviously her aunt, Mrs Hunter. To put it briefly, the story is of two youthful tragedies happily averted and turned into merriment: Henry Vane tried to drown Peggy Smart in a huge tub of water, and Kit Smart and little Anne attempted to elope together. So far, if the story shows a flaw in any-body's character, it would seem to be in Henry's. But there is more. Mrs Le Noir adds that some verses in the 1791 edition were written for Anne Vane by Kit when he was only thirteen: "To Ethelinda—on her doing my verses the honour of wearing them in her bosom." Christopher Hunter con-firms the story, so it had better be accepted—though it seems possible that the printed verses were later than those that were actually put in the bosom of the eleven-year-old Anne. There are four stanzas, but one will be sufficient:

Oft thro' my eyes my soul has flown
And wanton'd on that ivory throne:
There with extatic transport burn'd
And thought it was to heav'n return'd.
Tell me, is the omen true,
Shall the body follow too?

Critics who take a poor view of Smart's character have found in these lines "a voluptuousness of mind somewhat startling in a thirteen-year-old boy" and that "there is about the piece a warmth of passion uncomfortable, whether arti-ficial or not." On the other hand they tend to agree that dis-appointment in this youthful love-affair (Anne Vane married

Charles Hope Weir in 1746) may have "precipitated Smart on his career of dissipation," a natural result when "a great love has been stricken by despair."

But in fact I do not think Smart either caused or sustained any damage, only a pleasurable impression which, as the years went on became something rare and spiritual. Poetry, not passion, is the key to this affair: imitation poetry at the beginning and genuine poetry at the end. Smart was precocious in trivialities, but slow and deep of growth in the things that mattered.

At thirteen, already determined to be a poet, he found himself "in love"; he had to express his "passion." The honeyed impudences of Elizabethans and Cavaliers—or perhaps directly his own Horace and Catullus—were the only models he knew. The result was an exercise in bad taste, but the style was creditably taut and economic.

It would be absurd to conduct an inquisition on a two-centuries-old children's love-affair, were it not that Smart kept remembering this girl twenty-five years later when he was in deep adversity. At least he kept remembering *his idea* of the girl. So it is worth reconstructing the affair from what happened at the time and from what happened afterwards.

What happened—or rather, what did *not* happen—was that Christopher did nothing to impair the friendly goodwill of all the Vanes towards him and nothing to impair his own studious application to his books which got him into Cambridge. So the most likely reality is that Anne enjoyed playing the part of a Captive Princess or a Lady of Fashion, and Christopher was commandeered to be her knight-errant or her "servant"—*cavaliere serviente*. He very much enjoyed the experience; it coincided with awakening adolescence and it gave him confidence. Moreover Anne represented, however much in miniature, the fairy-tale world of noble castles; he felt the thrill, partly ambitious, partly chivalrous, which every honourable middle-class youth must feel at being intimately trusted by a *domina castellana*. It must be remembered that until he went to Cambridge Smart had never entered that peculiarly brilliant but tarnished world which

27

we call "the eighteenth century"; his upbringing had been in an older England, stoutly rural, softly feudal, immemorial.

As the years went on and Lord Barnard became the Earl of Darlington, and his daughter became Lady Anne Hope Weir and then (after a sad divorce case) Lady Anne Monson, a charming and malicious woman of the world, relations with Smart remained those of noble patrons towards a respectful client.

> Can I forget fair Raby's towers,
>   How awful and how great!
> Can I forget such blissful bowers,
>   Such splendour in retreat!
>
> Where me, ev'n me, an infant bard,
> Cleveland and Hope indulgent heard . . .
> *Hope*, copyist of her mother's mind,
> Is loveliest, liveliest of her kind,
>   Her soul with every virtue teems.

—he wrote in one of the many poems dedicated to Lord Barnard. But the ideal Anne continued to grow up separately in some tower of ivory and came to comfort him, bearing her first married name, when he was in the madhouse in 1760:

> I bless God for two visions of Anne Hope's being in charity with me.

Anyone who knows Smart's ineradicable clinging to wordplay will understand why the vision was under her married name. Gratitude and Hope—"the Seraph and his spouse" were the two powers or virtues that sustained him to the end of his life. She was also probably responsible for two lines whose beauty is almost unearthly:

> For I saw a blush in Staindrop Church, which was of God's own colouring,
>   For it was the benevolence of a virgin shewn to me before the whole congregation.

Staindrop was the village near Raby Castle. It was here, near the original home of the Smart family, that Christopher had dreamed of the ancestral estate where he would spend his declining years in ease and good fellowship with all. But the nearest he was to get to it was the room in the madhouse where he had the vision of Staindrop;[1] and thereafter, in the same room, he made the resolution that he must wait till eternity for his true homecoming:

> For my grounds in New Canaan shall infinitely compensate for the flats & maynes of Staindrop Moor.

Well, the first stage in the journey from Staindrop to the room whence he looked back at Staindrop was when he entered Pembroke Hall, Cambridge, on 30 October 1739, aged seventeen.

The £40 he had from the Duchess was a generous sum, but it was almost all he had; it was not nearly enough to put him in the same class as the "Fellow Commoners"—sons of the nobility and squirearchy who had come up to Cambridge mostly for sport and excitement. So naturally he took his place—as Edmund Spenser had done before him—among the "Sizars," that is, the poorer boys who paid off part of their fees by doing work such as washing up and waiting on the Fellow Commoners. The system was an old-established one. Smart may have meditated ruefully the contrast between his subservience to these wealthy boors at Cambridge and his easy familiarity with the noble imps of Raby Castle. But the system helped him at least to do some serious bookwork—a practice unheard of amongst the Fellow Commoners.

His Tripos Latin verses each year were thought exceptionally good (so his nephew tells us) and worth printing; eventually in 1742 he won the Craven scholarship, open to all undergraduates, with a Latin translation of Pope's *Ode on Saint Cecilia's Day*. The scholarship brought him an

---

[1] Mr Geoffrey Grigson in his pamphlet *Christopher Smart* gives a brilliantly detailed example of this mental vision of Staindrop Moor which explains the attractive but mysterious lines in *A Song to David*:

> The grass the polyanthus cheques;
> And polish'd porphyry reflects
> By the descending rill.

"Anyone who knows," he writes, "the limestone country of Raby and of Staindrop Moor . . . will at once see the flower and the rock and the waterfall in a characteristic conjunction in the limestone so finely polished by centuries of the descending rill, protruding from grass checquered with the lilac umbels, by the thousand, of the Birdseye Primrose."

extra £20 a year in money; but its real value for Smart was that it procured him an introduction to Mr Pope himself. Pope wrote him a very civil letter (the introduction was effected by Mr Murray, afterwards Lord Mansfield) of thanks and congratulations in 1743, with suggestions for further translations. This led to a meeting at Twickenham in 1744, not long before Pope's death.

Pope's regard meant a very great deal to Smart. When his portrait was painted some years later, he is shown, pen in hand, with the hand resting upon Pope's letter. And in 1754, when he was introducing his friend Tom Tyers to Samuel Johnson, and Johnson had recited a psalm which he had just put into Latin verse, "Smart in return," continues Tom Tyers, "recited some of his own Latin compositions; he had translated with success, and to Mr Pope's *satisfaction*, his St Cecilian ode." It was not the only time Smart had mentioned Pope's approval in the intervening ten years. Its importance for him at the time was that it gave him the recognition he had been starved of in the last few years, recognition as a poet and as a person.

Cambridge during the past four years, 1739-43, had been rather like a long, dark tunnel to him. When he turned from the hardships of a sizar's life to bury himself in his books, he found that his progress there brought little recognition from the authorities. The classics were held in low esteem at that time in Cambridge; mathematics was the only school which enjoyed any prestige. Smart possessed his soul in patience; but his early poems show that a very well-defined personality was taking shape, ready to burst out when the time came. While his brain was working efficiently at his studies, he was whispering to himself in his early ode on *Idleness*:

> Sister of peace and indolence,
>   Bring, Muse, bring numbers soft and slow;
> Elaborately void of sense,
>   And sweetly thoughtless let them flow . . .

> For thee, O Idleness, the woes
>   Of life, we patiently endure.
> Thou art the source whence labour flows,
>   We shun thee but to make thee sure.

Smart, however, was not an idler. "Idleness" was just a temporary name he gave to the goddess whom he really worshipped under the more accurate names of "Good Nature," or, alternatively, "Innocence." He meant the paradisal faculty of being able to adore divine beauty without disobedience to God's will. One of the Cambridge Platonists, Henry More, may have helped him to know what he meant.

Wherefore God indued the Soul of Man with a Faculty of being united with vital joy and complacency to the Matter, as well as of aspiring to an Union with God himself, whose Divine Essence is too highly disproportioned to our poor substances. But the Divine Life is communicable in some sort to both Soul and Body . . . and those wonderful grateful pleasures that we feel are nothing but the kindly motions of the Soul's *Vehicle*; from whence Divine joyes themselves are by a kind of reflexion strengthened and advanced. Of so great consequence is that Vital principle that joyns the Soul to the Matter of the Universe.

This vital aptitude in the Soul of being united with corporeal Matter being so essential to her and proper, the invigorating the exercise of that Faculty cannot but be very grateful and acceptable to her, and a very considerable share of her happinesse. Else what means the *Resurrection of the dead* or *Bodies* in the other world? which yet is an Article of the Christian Faith. . . . This is the *Feminine Faculty* in the Soul of Man, which awakes then earliest into act, when the Soul to *Intellectuals* falls asleep.

It was a brisk faculty, quite the opposite of idleness or apathy, as he explained in his ode *On Good Nature*:

No—thou art active—spirit all—
Swifter than lightning at the call
    Of injur'd innocence, or griev'd desert,
    And large with liberality's thy heart.

Thy appetites in easy tides
(As reason's luminary guides)
    Soft flow—no wind can work them to a storm,
    Correctly quick, dispassionately warm.

Yet if a transport thou canst feel
'Tis only for thy neighbours weal:
    Great, generous acts thy ductile passions move,
    And smilingly thou weep'st with joy and love . . .

Extensive, as from west to east,
Thy love descends from man to beast,
    Nought is excluded, little, or infirm,
    Thou canst with greatness stoop to save a worm.

Come, goddess, come with all thy charms,
For Oh! I love thee, to my arms—
    All, all my actions guide, my fancy feed,
So shall *existence* then be *life* indeed.

This was Smart in what we may call his natural verse, rural and personal. But even at this early date he was already beginning to write his artificial verse, urban and social. He was already gaining a reputation for wit which only needed opportunity to become fame. He took some part in the limited and oafish amusements that were available to the sizars; there are some lines on the popular and meretricious barmaid at the Mitre which are of interest because their date can be fixed as 1741, when he was nineteen. There is in them one line of poetry, which might have come straight from Andrew Marvell (who, as I have said, I think was his early model), "Markt, little hemispheres, with stars"; the rest is all in that wry, facetious, self-mocking style which was to grow on him increasingly, ending always hollowly with "a false conclusion . . . like an unfilled can."

No handkerchief her bosom hid,
    No tippet from our sight debars
Her heaving breasts with moles o'erspread
    Markt, little hemispheres, with stars;
While on them all our eyes we move,
Our eyes that meant immoderate love . . .

But hark, she cries, 'My mamma calls,'
    And strait she's vanish'd from our sight;
'Twas then we saw the empty bowls,
    'Twas then we first perceiv'd it night;
While all, sad synod, silent moan
Both that she went—and went alone.

There are three more of his poems at this time which I think a biographer must take into account. The first is a clever piece of self-expression. In some college court he came across an old eagle caged and neglected there. Smart was always inwardly angered by cruelty to animals, but in his youth he did not have the courage, or perhaps the full awareness of his convictions. He let his pity for the eagle make it a type of Greece and Rome, that is, of the classical studies despised at Cambridge, and at the same time was able to infuse into it his own sense of frustration.

> Oh cruel fate! what barbarous hand,
>   What more than *Gothic* ire,
> At some fierce tyrant's dread command,
>   To check thy daring fire,
> Has plac'd thee in this servile cell,
> Where Discipline and Dulness dwell . . .
>
> What time by thee scholastic Pride
> Takes his precise, pedantic stride,
>   Nor on thy mis'ry casts a care;
> The stream of love ne'er from his heart
> Flows out, to act fair pity's part;
>   But stinks, and stagnates there . . .
>
> Thou type of wit and sense confin'd,
> Cramp'd by the oppressors of the mind,
>   Who study downward on the ground;
> Type of the fall of *Greece* and *Rome*;
> While more than mathematic gloom,
>   Envelopes all around!

The next piece—inscribed on an Aeolian harp—is a very poor thing in itself, but valuable because it shows the continuity of his thought through periods long before and long after his first confinement for madness. The example of this instrument, on which the breezes blowing free could make mysterious music sweeter than any artificial touch, attracted him at once as a bright idea; but in fact it had to go through a long time of cocoon growth before its wings unfolded. For Smart, as I have said, was a person who took many years to discover the deep, grasping roots of the bright things that he snatched at.

The idea of the *Windflügel* or Aeolian Lyre—first described to Europeans by the Jesuit scientist Father Athanasius Kircher in 1650—seems to have been arousing interest at that time. Gray made use of it in the opening line of his Pindaric ode on the progress of poesy:

> Awake, Aeolian lyre, awake,
> And give to rapture all thy trembling strings . . .

Smart was caught by the idea much earlier, and also by the

story that King David used to hang his zither by his bed and listen to the midnight breezes playing on its strings. He inscribed some Latin verses on one side of an Aeolian harp and an English translation on the other:

> Hail, heav'nly harp, where Memnon's skill is shown,
> That charm'st the ear with music all thine own!
> Which, though untouch'd, can'st rapt'rous strains impart,
> O rich of genuine nature, free from art!
> Such the wild warblings of the sylvan throng,
> So simply sweet the untaught virgin's song.

But fifteen years later in the madhouse those trite undergraduate ideas had become these deeply pondered thoughts:

> For GOD the father Almighty plays upon the HARP of stupendous magnitude and melody.
> For innumerable Angels fly out at every touch and his tune is a work of creation.
> For at that time malignity ceases and the devils themselves are at peace.
> For this time is perceptible to man by a remarkable stillness and serenity of soul.
> For the Æolian harp is improveable into regularity . . .

Later still the inspiration finally bore fruit in the superb and majestic *Song to David*:

> For ADORATION on the strings
> The western breezes work their wings,
> The captive ear to soothe.—
> Hark! 'tis a voice—how still and small—
> That makes the cataracts to fall,
> Or bids the sea be smooth!

In these years, in his early twenties, Christopher was still feeling the pull of inspiration from wild nature, a pull as deep as his early childhood. But he was also feeling the pull of social success. In 1743 he came to the end of his long, dark tunnel when he celebrated his Bachelor's degree with a shout of joy. *On taking a Batchelor's Degree* is a neatly clever piece, a patchwork of applied quotations from Horace, until at the end he addresses his tailor:

> Meanwhile, friend BANKS, my merits claim
> Their just reward from you,
> For HORACE bids us challenge fame,
> When once that fame's our due,

34

> Invest me with a graduate's gown,
> Midst shouts of all beholders,
> My head with ample square-cap crown,
> And deck with hood my shoulders.

Two years later he was awarded his Fellowship. In the meantime he had obtained those commendations from Pope which were probably influential in securing the Fellowship. Armed with these, and with a little spare money at last to jingle in his purse, Christopher stepped out into a new world.

About the same time another young man of about the same age was beginning his adventures. In August 1745 Prince Charlie unfurled the royal standard at Glenfinnan. "GOD bless the House of Stuart" and "GOD be merciful to the House of STUART in their afflictions" wrote Smart in the latter days of his own afflictions. But at the time he was probably too occupied with himself to spare more than a passing thrill or a passing pang.

THREE

◆

Cambridge

SMART'S bow to the public as a newly-recognized wit and scholar was marked by his bursting into print with by far his most ambitious poem to date. This was a long *Ode to Musick* written by himself with a flowery preface for his readers and accompanied by his Latin translation of Pope's *Ode*. It was printed at Cambridge, but the fashionable bookseller, Robert Dodsley, had agreed to sell copies of it in London. At the same time Smart began to write for the *Museum*, a London periodical run by Dodsley and the poet Akenside; his contribution was a bantering love-verse, the first of a number of the same sort, devoted to a tall girl called Harriet, or Harriot, sister of his Cambridge friend Jermyn Pratt.

About the same time Thomas Gray bestirred himself and sent up three of his early *Odes* to be published (anonymously) in Dodsley's Miscellany. Perhaps Smart's success had piqued him; for hitherto Gray had taken the view that a gentleman should not hawk his poems about to find a buyer. These *Odes*—on *Spring*, *Eton College* and *Adversity*—had been written five years earlier; since then, Gray's muse seemed to have deserted him completely; another four years were to elapse before the *Elegy* was written. It so happens that most of our information about the next year in Smart's life, a very important one, 1747, comes from the scratchy, rather spiteful, rather pathetic pen of Thomas Gray.

There is no doubt that Smart irritated Gray. They should really have been friends these two, authors of the two greatest poems of the mid-century; they were living in the same college; they both venerated the classics and detested the "mathematic gloom" of Cambridge; they both had the same attraction to "Welsh-ness" and to wild nature. But two strong barriers kept them apart, one of circumstance, the other of temperament.

Gray was six years Smart's senior in age and one year his junior in academic preferment. After matriculating at Peterhouse in 1734 he had deserted Cambridge and spent several years touring the continent with his fashionable friend Horace Walpole, son of the Prime Minister. In 1742 he returned, with somewhat ungracious condescension, to Peterhouse as a Fellow Commoner and took a law degree two years later. But he found the boisterous youths of Peterhouse altogether too much for him. In 1746 he was practically living at Pembroke with his friend Thomas Warton, and was taking a surprising interest in the internal affairs and minor scandals of the college. There may have been a sharper point to his irritation if the story of Smart's witticism against him is true. Gray was not a popular figure. Although he affected to despise the dons, he had himself a very precise and pedantic manner; he walked with mincing steps, one hand holding up his gown behind, and a supercilious expression on his face. "Gray *walks* as if he had fouled his small-clothes, and *looks* as if he smelt it" was the coarse and cruel gibe ascribed to Christopher Smart in *Facetiae Cantabrigienses*. Whether he really made it or whether it came to Gray's ears, we do not know for certain. But it is certain that something in Smart stung Gray to a good many adverse comments, and these comments give us a useful picture of Smart as he stood preening himself for the first time in the sunlight of public applause.

Gray saw a commonplace-looking little fellow with stubby features and a tubby shape; but his eyes and his mouth were extremely expressive and they were nearly always at work expressing something. There was no doubt the man was witty; one day when it was realized that all the three University Beadles were very fat men, Smart was the first to exploit it in a flash with:

Pinguia tergeminorum—abdomina Bedellorum.

But he was ridiculously proud of Pope's purely conventional compliments, and was setting himself up already as the poet-laureate of Cambridge. He had written the Ode for the Jubilee of Pembroke and was to be chosen to compose the official University praises of King George II. Then, this very year 1746, out he came again with his Latin prize poem, accompanied this time by a long English effusion of his own on Saint Cecilia, to be set to music: the same subject that had already been exhausted by the great efforts of John Dryden and Alexander Pope.

As Gray scanned young Smart's preface to the poem, he found it was an answer to all his own objections about a scribbler trying to emulate Pope and Dryden. Smart wrote it (he said) simply to oblige a much-respected musical friend who wanted to exercise his talents on the lines and also to exercise himself in the *Pindaric* mood, a mood "which should consist in the vehemence of sudden and unlooked-for transitions: hence chiefly it derives that enthusiastic fire and wildness which greatly distinguishes it from other species of Poesy."

He certainly did show remarkable imitative skill in his "sudden and unlooked-for transitions" from one style to another: the secret musings of Marvell:

> In all the woods, in all the plains
> Around a lively stillness reigns;
> The deer approach the secret scene,
> And weave their way thro' labyrinths green;
> While *Philomela* learns the lay,
> And answers from the neighbouring bay.

the soothing magic of the early Milton:

> He sung—The winds are charm'd to sleep,
> Soft stillness steals along the deep,
>   The *Tritons* and the *Nereids* sigh
>   In soul-reflecting sympathy,
> And all the audience of waters weep.

and the strong lines of Dryden in Smart's praises of Purcell, "mellifluous, yet manly too":

> Not like the soft *Italian* swains
> He trills the weak enervate strains,
>   Where sense and musick are at strife;
> His vigorous notes with meaning teem,
> With fire, with force explain the theme,
>   And sing the subject into life.

But was it all copying? There were some passages where Smart seemed to have his own music and his own peculiar ideas, for example about the "ductile passions," a phrase already used in his ode *On Good Nature*.

> But o'er th' affections too she claims the sway,
> Pierces the human heart, and steals the soul away,
> And as attractive sounds move high or low,
> Th' obedient ductile passions ebb and flow.
> Has any nymph her faithful lover lost,
>   And in the visions of the night
>   And all the day-dreams of the light,
> In sorrows' tempest turbulently tost . . .
> She too shall sympathize, she till shall moan,
> And pitying others' sorrows sigh away her own.

Gray was too honest a poet not to recognize here a master of rhythm, nearly, if not quite, equal to himself. Part of his anger with Smart was not jealousy but honest indignation at the way Smart seemed to be squandering his talents. He had become tutor to young Mr Delaval (a coveted and much-intrigued-for post) and seemed to think that this entitled him to standards of noble extravagance; his frequent changes of fine linen and his embroidered waistcoats were clearly, Gray thought, beyond his means. And he was wasting his time on a low and ridiculous stage-comedy. The following letter written by Gray to his friend Thomas Warton in March 1747 is an interesting mixture of genuine concern and rankling jealousy; it is a question which motive it was that inspired the shockingly accurate forecast in the last sentence:

As to Smart he must necessarily be *abîmé* in a short time. His debts daily increase (you remember the state they were in when you left us). Addison, I know, wrote smartly to him last week; but it has had no effect that signifies, only I observe he takes hartshorn from morning to night lately: in the meantime he is amusing himself with a comedy of his own writing, which he makes all the boys of his acquaintance act, and intends to borrow the Zodiac room and have it performed publickly. Our friend Lawman, the mad attorney, is his copyist; and truly the author himself is as mad as he. His piece (he says) is inimitable, true sterling wit and humour, by God; and he cant hear the Prologue without being ready to die with laughter. He acts five parts himself and is only sorry he cant do all the rest. He has also advertised a collection of Odes; and for his Vanity and Faculty of Lying, they are come to their full maturity. All this, you see, must come to a Jayl, or Bedlam, and that without any help, almost without pity.

There is no doubt that Smart was throwing his money wildly about. Hunter, who on the whole is tender to his uncle's memory, says: "The civilities shown him by persons greatly his superiors in rank and character, either induced him to expect mines of wealth from the exertions of his talents, or encouraged him to think himself exempted from attention to common obligations." Low company seems to have been as fatal to his finances as high society. Whether from foolish vanity or from extravagant good-fellowship, he seemed unable to resist the opportunity to stand a drink and crack a joke. An early sketch of him by his friend Charles Burney recalls:

While he was the pride of Cambridge and the chief poetical ornament of that University, he ruined himself by returning the tavern treats of strangers who had invited him as a wit and an extraordinary personage, in order to boast of his acquaintance. This social spirit of retaliation, involving him in debt with vintners and college cooks, occasioned his fellowship to be sequestered, obliged him to quit the university, and crippled him for the rest of his life.

But, as a matter of fact, Burney, who was not at Cambridge, is here painting too black a picture. It was several years after Smart had left Cambridge voluntarily that his fellowship was reluctantly taken away from him, and then only because his marriage made it inevitable; and even then his name was kept on the books.

Indeed, if we look at Smart, not with wisdom-after-the-event across the shadows of gaol and bedlam, nor with the gloomy prescience of Gray, but through the eyes of his numerous friendly contemporaries, we get a completely different picture. Debts and drinking were failings common to young men; what distinguished Smart was his merriment in his cups and his generosity to others in his expenditure. There is no doubt that he thoroughly enjoyed himself and communicated a lot of enjoyment to other people. He was no squalid dipsomaniac. The affair of the Comedy, if nothing else, is sufficient to prove that. You cannot write, produce and play a part in a successful comedy, and be a dipsomaniac at the same time; you could do one of the three perhaps—and indeed it has been done—but not all three together.

The affair of Smart's Comedy is worth going into a little more deeply. For one thing, it obliges us to dismiss about half Gray's letter as nonsense motivated by malice, either general or particular. It was a perfectly straightforward comedy, the sort of thing you would expect between Farquhar and Sheridan, and it is a pity that the text has not survived. The plot concerns a plethoric Baronet travelling to Cambridge with his beautiful niece to interview his foolish nephew, a Fellow Commoner of Trinity. On the way, the carriage being stuck in a flood, the party is rescued by a poor young student from Emmanuel who falls reciprocally in love with the niece, but the gap between their stations seems too great for hope. Arrived at Cambridge, the Baronet is flattered into taking part in some theatricals, during which, in his character as a magistrate, he unwittingly signs his consent to the marriage and the surrender of the niece's fortune: obviously plenty of opportunities for excellent fooling.

Smart took the part of the Baronet. There were ten other members of the cast, nearly all of whom subsequently became most respectable clergymen: archdeacons, precentors, prebendaries and so forth; and at least three of them, Stonhewer, Gordon and Randall the organist (who wrote the music for the St Cecilia Ode) remained good friends to Smart throughout his period of adversity. Hunter got his information about the comedy from "an eminent person who was an actor in it" and it is clear from the eminent person's account that he retained proud and pleasant memories of the enterprise. It was acted in Pembroke Hall, and among the audience were evidently Mr Jermyn Pratt and his sprightly sister "Harriot," for Smart's prologue includes these lines:

41

> Whene'er immortal Shakespeare's works are read,
> He wins the heart before he strikes the head.
> Swift to the soul the piercing image flies,
> Swifter than *Harriot's* wit, or *Harriot's* eyes.

Smart wrote a number of poems to Harriot during these years. The general tone of them indicates that they were an occasion of good humour rather than heart-burning on either side. Smart was a shocking flatterer. (Shortly before his death, long after he had ceased to take any interest in women, he could not resist paying outrageous compliments to seventeen-year-old Fanny Burney, just to please and flatter her in the looser convention of that age.) Harriot was probably the tall girl whom he addressed in a poem which is of interest, I think, because it refutes the suggestion that Smart's small size gave him an inferiority feeling which led to persecution-mania. The poet is obviously chuckling when he begs her, before she yields to some gigantic youth, to reason with herself:

> Say, is it carnage makes the man?
> Is to be monstrous really to be great?
> Say, is it wise or just to scan
> Your lover's worth by quantity or weight?
> Ask your mamma and nurse if it be so;
> Nurse and mamma I ween shall jointly answer, no.

The last line of another verse suggests that his smallness may have helped him to have that "miniaturist's eye" which Mr Callan has noticed in his poetry:

> Look in the glass, survey that cheek—
> Where FLORA has with all her roses blush'd;
> The shape so tender,—look so meek—
> The breasts made to be press'd, not to be crush'd—
> Then turn to me,—turn with obliging eyes,
> Nor longer nature's works, in miniature, despise.

Another charge levelled at Smart by recent biographers—that of "sycophancy"—seems to come from a similar misreading of his character. Smart, as has been said, was a born flatterer, but he was no sycophant; he just intensely wanted to please and to make others happy; he flattered individuals both high and low, humble middle-class folk as well as noble

42

lords; but those who became his friends, whether simple or gentle, never treated him as a sycophant is treated. A good example of this is his pupil at Cambridge, young Mr Delaval.

There was a good deal of envy and intrigue about who should be young Delaval's tutor; but it seems quite clear from Gray's letters that Smart was no party to the intrigues, though he may have been their beneficiary. It was regrettably common at that time for tutors to be toadies and panders to the vices of their charges in the hope of profit or preferment. But such was evidently *not* the relationship between Smart and young Delaval. He was his tutor only for a very short time; for in the same year (1746) Delaval was finally sent down for smuggling a girl into his rooms disguised as an officer. Yet long after, when he had sown his wild oats and become Lord Delaval, he retained for Smart an affection which one would not have for a toady or a pander; and when a subscription was being got up for Smart after his escape from confinement in 1763, all the Delaval family rallied round to support him.

So in these last years at Cambridge, as throughout his whole life, Smart presents us with two outstanding characteristics: his complete inability to manage his finances, and his extraordinary faculty for inspiring friendship for his own sake. Both are interesting clues to his real nature.

Hunter attributed the first to insobriety. But it surely went deeper than that. There was a lack in Smart, drunk or sober, which was like a throwback to a more ancient way of living. You get it in peoples like the Bantu who are (or were till recently) complete strangers to the idea of monetary value; to them saving money and putting a fixed price on anything seem positively evil actions, destructive of good fellowship and civilized society as they conceive it. Smart had this same deep, almost unconquerable repugnance to money values. The adjective "Franciscan" comes to mind again, but one must be careful as yet about the use of it.

The counterpoise of this lack was that, with all idea of money value washed clean out of his mind, he was able to see things and people in brighter and more lovely colours than they appeared to others. That was why he seemed to flatter people. He did indeed flatter them; he let them see themselves as he saw them, and they were attracted to him as cold and weary travellers to a warm and friendly fire. He radiated happiness, and that was a quality which even in that venal age made any mere quantity seem little by comparison. Indeed it is surprising in the brutal eighteenth century how many examples one comes across in worldly people of clean disinterested charity and goodness.

Smart's creditors caught up with him in November 1747. The first was a tailor to whom he had a long-standing debt of £50; after that they all pounced. According to Gray's careful computation the total debit was £350. The other Fellows rallied round and kept him in hiding till they could persuade the creditors to accept a composite instalment of £50 a year. Smart's income (Gray reckoned) was over £140 a year as long as he kept on living at Cambridge. Gray's letter is interesting for the precision of its numerical details and the self-evident absurdity of some of its judgments—for example that Smart's conduct had lost him *"his only friend,"* whereas it is obvious he abounded in friends:

Your mention of Mr. Vane remains me of poor Smart (not that I or any mortal pity him). About three weeks ago he was arrested here at the suit of a Taylor in London for a debt of about £50 of three years standing. The College had about £28 due to him in their hands, the rest (to hinder him from going to the Castle,[1] for he could not raise a shilling) Brown, May and Peele lent him upon his note. Upon this he remained confined to his rooms lest his creditors here should snap him; and the fellows sent round to make out a list of his debts, which amounted in Cambridge to above £350; that they might come the readier to some composition, he was advised to go off in the night and lie hid somewhere or other. He has done so, and this has made the creditors agree to an assignment of £50 per annum out of his income, which is above £140, if he lives at Cambridge (not else). But I am apprehensive, if this comes to the ears of Mr. Vane he may take away the £40 hitherto allowed him by the Duke of Cleveland; for before all this (last summer) I know they talked of doing so, as Mr. Smart (they said) was settled in the world. If you found an opportunity possibly you might hinder this (which would totally ruin him now) by representing his absurdity in the best light it will bear; but at the same time they should make this a condition of its continuance; that he live in college, soberly, and within bounds, for that upon any information to the contrary it shall be absolutely stopped. This would

[1] i.e. the prison.

be doing him a real service, though against the grain: yet I must own, if you heard all his lies, impertinence and ingratitude in this affair, it would perhaps quite set you against him, as it has his only friend (Mr. Addison)[1] totally. And yet one would try to save him, for drunkenness is one great source of all this, and he may change it. I would not tell this matter in the north, if I were you, till I found it was known by other means.

It is clear that everyone was anxious to save Smart—including Gray himself. He was writing to Thomas Warton, who was living at Durham, and his anxiety about the Vane allowance of £40 seems a little officious and overdone. It was in fact continued as long as Smart remained at Cambridge.

He remained for two more years, and he does not seem to have been under the shadow of any disgrace. He became Master of Arts in 1747 and wrote the Ode to the King in 1748. Then, halfway through 1749, he took a decision which had probably been in his mind for a long time. He left Cambridge to begin the life of a writer in London.

His nephew Hunter and his friend Burney both regarded this as the fatal mistake which upset his career; and recent biographers have seen in it the first great example of his "ruinous weakness of will." There is a great deal to be said for the view that he made a mistake—that he was more designed by nature to be an ornament of the university than a London business-man—but there is nothing to be said for the opinion of recent biographers that it was a case of "ruinous weakness of will." On the contrary, it took a strong and lively will—which Smart undoubtedly possessed—to disengage himself from the groove of easy security and step out into the unknown. The choice was between servitude with comfort on the one hand and poverty with freedom on the other; and he made his choice deliberately.

"Servitude" may seem too harsh a term for the mild dominion of Cambridge over its children; but it must be remembered that the trappings of monasticism still clung to a Fellow's life; it was exposed to the obloquy attaching to Roman Catholic monasticism without the corresponding spiritual advantages. Let us hear a contemporary man-of-the-world opinion:

[1] Smart's former tutor.

45

Gluttony therefore and idleness are both to be added to the remoter causes of Consequential Madness. . . . To the second, perhaps more than to a spirit of lying may be ascribed the temptations of St. Anthony and the lazy monks his followers, the extasies of sedentary and chlorotic Nuns, and their frequent conversations with Angelic ministers of grace. Not to mention what now and then happens to the Senior Recluses in our Protestant Monasteries at *Oxford* and *Cambridge*.

This was written while Gibbon was still a schoolboy by a gentleman called Dr Battie, an authority on lunatics, whom we shall meet again later on. Smart had a genuine piety and a deep interest in religion; but it was the very depth and piety of his nature that made him shrink from becoming a worldly recluse. He showed the strength and liveliness of his will when he left Cambridge for London. On the other hand, it must be stressed that it was a purely selfish decision. He was destined to become a great religious poet and, in the end, to identify himself with the poor and suffering. But both these aspirations were smothered when he went to London. He blunted his sensitivity both morally and as a poet.

As a poet during these years he never fulfilled the beautiful promise of his English St Cecilia Ode—which can be judged by the extracts at the beginning of this chapter. In the preface to that ode he had written, very interestingly, of his ambition to write a great poem on the theme of David playing his harp to soothe Saul. But many strange things were to happen before he fulfilled that destined task. Meanwhile he had not given up his poetic ambitions. But his two major efforts, *The Hop-Garden* (about 700 lines) and *The Rural Day* were both spoiled by self-consciousness. *The Hop-Garden* has many pretty phrases coming back from his Kentish childhood, but it is written in sloppy "Miltonic" blank verse; and, in his imitations of Virgil's Georgics, he cannot make up his mind whether to be serious or burlesque. *The Rural Day*, consisting of Morning, Noon and Night pieces, is more successful; it was printed in the *London Magazine* of 1748; the tight rhyme-schemes and light cadences in it are much more suited to Smart's talent than blank verse could be. The Morning piece had some strong lines much admired by Goldsmith, but the other two tail off into improprieties which are neither here nor there. Smart had several other

46

poems published at this time, in the *London Magazine* or in Dodsley's *Museum*, mostly half-comic love-poems to "Harriot." There is no doubt he had opened a way for himself to be a successful poet, but he seemed to have closed the way to being a great poet.

Morally, too, he had slipped, if Hunter was speaking for his family when he wrote of Smart exempting himself "from attention to common obligations." He was the breadwinner; his income at Cambridge had been helped by efforts and sacrifices at home; it was his duty to help his mother to get his two sisters settled. That is not to mention the number of poor tradesmen and artisans whose families may have suffered through his unpaid debts. On the whole he had probably enough to justify his wave of repentance seven years later.

It is pleasant to end this chapter by recording the generosity with which Cambridge, his *Alma Mater*, treated him. The authorities did not deprive him of his Fellowship and they kept voting him supplies of ten or twelve pounds every year from 1750 till 1752, "in lieu of commons." Only when his marriage became publicly known in 1753 were they obliged to withdraw his Fellowship. Even then his college kept his name on its books so that he could go on competing for a certain religious prize poem which began in 1750. It was these religious poems which served, as will be seen, to keep Smart in touch with the deeper and more genuine part of his poetic talent. They also—perhaps paradoxically—kept him in touch with respectability. For the rest, he had chosen to live by his wits.

FOUR

London

LITERARY London where Smart was now venturing to seek his fortune had fallen sadly from the high days of Swift and Addison. David Hume, the philosopher, *en route* from Edinburgh to Paris, by-passed it with a superior sniff: "I have a reluctance to think of living among the factious barbarians of the Thames. Letters are there held in no honour."

The blame for this low repute is generally laid on the ample shoulders of Sir Robert Walpole and the Pelhams. In the days of Good Queen Anne—so the lamentation ran—both Whigs and Tories were prepared to pay for the very best in literary propaganda; the great writers of the day were active politicians; they gave their services wholeheartedly to their respective parties and shared equally in the hardships and rewards. But the long reign of Walpole saw the end of that. If Walpole wanted literary propaganda, he was content to pay third- and fourth-rate hacks to supply it in the form of scurrility and abuse.

Wherever the blame may be assigned, London in 1749 certainly pullulated with a swarm of half-baked periodicals and half-educated authors whose names are hardly known today outside the British Museum, an underworld of Hills and Kenricks and Pilkingtons and Hiffernans whose stock-in-trade, as Goldsmith said, was "to be very abusive and very dull." There were probably not many more readers than there were writers.

Indeed that was the real problem from an economic point

of view. The age of discerning patronage was over, and the age of the large reading public had not yet begun. The intervening gap was filled by the "booksellers," whose bookselling was often quite a minor branch of their activities. They ranged from informal literary agents, cheerful improvident souls who sank or swam with their authors, to big businessmen who paid by the page irrespective of literary talent, and what they usually paid for was advertisement, palate-tickling and literary stunts. The decade 1750–60 was when the booksellers reigned supreme. Men of literary genius like Fielding and Johnson managed to keep their heads above water either because they had some independent status —Fielding was a magistrate—or, like Johnson, by a proud and courageous devotion to their craft.

It was Johnson, in fact, who lifted letters back to a place of honour by the sheer force of his personality. He knocked a bookseller down with a folio as single-mindedly as he demolished Lord Chesterfield with a famous blast of prose— the letter which he epitomized in a spoken sentence: "What, have I sailed a long and difficult journey round the world of English language, and does he *now* send out his cock-boat to tow me into harbour?" After this letter, and the dictionary which occasioned it, to belong to Johnson's circle began to be quite as great an honour as to be received at court. But by that time Smart had disappeared.

How good it would have been for him if he could have attached himself to a man of principle like Johnson. Already he had a high regard for him; both had received the commendation of Mr Pope, and it was Smart (Burney tells us) who first began to praise *The Rambler* when it appeared in early 1750. But at that time Johnson himself was still a lone and insignificant figure. Henry Fielding, if anyone, was reckoned to be the champion of literary talent against dullness.

This introduction, sketchy as it is, will help to explain the spiritual ailment which beset Smart in London despite his measure of success; for most of his success had to be achieved in violation of his natural bent towards poetry, learning and contemplation.

Success, in fact, came to him fairly quickly, in spite of an initial setback. He got no change out of Robert Dodsley, whom he had hoped for as a publisher of his collected poems. But at Vauxhall Gardens, where he had already established a foothold while at Cambridge, he quickly made friends. Vauxhall Gardens, owned by Jonathan Tyers, a Swiss immigrant, was the chief place in London for musical entertainment. (Tom Tyers, Jonathan's son, was the friend mentioned in Chapter Two whom Smart introduced to Johnson.) Through Boyce, the Cambridge organist, he had met Dr Arne, who ran the musical entertainment at the gardens, and Arne commissioned several of his poems to be set to airs. Here too he had met Arne's pupil, Charles Burney, the future historian of music, who remained devoted to Smart to the very end—though ill-health obliged him to leave London for Norfolk the following year and he did not return till 1760. Other lifelong friends from these early days in London were two pleasant, impecunious script-writers, Richard Rolt and Arthur Murphy; we must not, however, bracket these two without marking the gradation between them; Dr. Johnson never acknowledged Rolt's existence ("I have just come from Sam Johnson," said Rolt. . . . "Sir," said Johnson, "I never knew the man"); but Murphy, "Dear Mur," was one of his intimates.

We do not know exactly how Smart maintained himself during that winter, but in the spring of 1750 his fortunes took a sharp upward turn. On 25 March the Vice-Chancellor of Cambridge and the Master of Clare awarded him the Seatonian prize of £30 for his long poem on *The Eternity of the Supreme Being*, and commanded it to be printed. This award has already been mentioned, but not its origin. The worthy Mr Seaton bequeathed his estate to Cambridge to found and maintain a yearly prize open to all graduates for the best poem upon "one or other of the Perfections or Attributes of the Supreme Being, and so the succeeding years, till the subject is exhausted; and afterwards the Subject shall be either Death, Judgment, Heaven, Hell, Purity of Heart, &c., or whatever else may be judged by the Vice-Chancellor, Master of Clare Hall, or Greek Professor to be most conducive to the honour of the Supreme Being and recommendation of virtue."

One feels obliged to apportion admiration in three lots; to Mr Seaton for his altruism, to the Cambridge authorities for their encouragement of Smart, and to Smart himself who won the prize not only in 1750, the year it started, but every other year that he entered for it. What strikes one at first about the poem is the very slipshod blank verse in which it is written, but what strikes one later, on closer examination, is the intimate ease and genuine fervour with which Smart handles his difficult and abstract subject. It is the very opposite of a "set piece" hammered out to order. Smart shows a remarkable gift for putting theological truths into vivid and sometimes beautiful language. Particularly fascinating in this and subsequent prize-poems is the way in which images and concepts peculiar to himself will be brought to life again in the much later and greater *Song to David*. Two examples in this 1750 poem are "The two prime Pillars of the Universe, Creation and Redemption," and "That prop the painted chambers of the heavens." A later chapter on the *Song to David* will show that here are the rudiments of ideas that went to make up the very abstruse stanzas on the seven pillars of wisdom. We know that the idea of *A Song to David* came to Smart as early as 1746. We know that his St Cecilia Ode of that year gave evidence of a true vein of poetry. We know now from his Seatonian poems that he had a natural bent for metaphysical religious verse long before he developed religious mania. How a man who was so at ease with his religion could have become a religious maniac is a query that will have to be answered later. At present all that is to be noted is the way he could keep his own secret ideas revolving in his mind for so long while he was engaged in a whirlwind of quite alien activities.

The whirlwind appeared forthwith in the shape of a "bustling, multifarious, not unkindly, essentially commercial, essentially enterprising personage" named Mr John Newbery, whom Johnson called Jack Whirler, "who cannot stand still because he is wanted in another place, and who is wanted in many places because he stays in none." Newbery was a comparatively recent but rapidly expanding power in the bookselling and literary world. More details will be given about him when it is related how Smart became a member of his household. For the moment all that need be said is that he was the direct opposite of the typical "bad" bookseller. The typically wicked bookseller was the callous, cantankerous, bloodsucking Griffiths, owner of the Whig *Monthly Review*, in whose clutches poor Goldsmith writhed for so long. Newbery was "essentially commercial, essentially enterprising," as in Austin Dobson's description quoted above, but he was also genial and generous, with a shrewd appreciation of good literature—"a projecting head, good taste and great industry," Arthur Murphy described him.

One of Newbery's main industries was selling patent medicines, and his prize item among a galaxy of drops and lotions was the fever-powder of the celebrated Dr James, Johnson's friend and schoolfellow. His other main line was the writing and publication of children's story-books, a well-known series, *Goody Two Shoes, Jack the Giant-Killer*, etc. Who did the actual writing of them is not clear, but they greatly helped Newbery's persistent purpose, which was to widen and increase the reading public. For this purpose he had already been on a rapid but effective sales-tour through the provinces. He also ran a London periodical called *The Student* (or *The Oxford Miscellany*); but this was not doing too well in 1750.

Already his busy mind was intent on a new publication which should catch the small but increasing circle of readers. What they wanted—he decided—was nonsense, but distinguished nonsense. Smart, the Cambridge wit and scholar and good companion, was the very man for the job. It is said to have been Burney who introduced them, or it may have been Johnson or Dr James. The two men took to each other from the start.

What Smart wanted primarily was someone to publish his collected poems. Newbery was prepared to do this, but naturally on his own terms. Smart at the outset was a little too academic for him; but he gradually drew him down to the required level. First he published Smart's *Horatian*

Canons of Friendship, an urbane and innocuous exercise in heroic couplets which, if compared with Johnson's *London*, reminds one how much of a rustic at heart Smart really was. Next, he made Smart a partner in *The Student*, which thereupon expanded its subtitle to *The Oxford and Cambridge Miscellany* (Bonnell Thornton was the Oxford contributor). Smart used *The Student* to publish several of his early Cambridge poems as well as some new songs and cantatas written for Vauxhall Gardens. But already by the summer of that year he and Newbery had hatched the plan of their new monthly magazine. Which of the two was more responsible for the hatching cannot be guessed, but what came out of the egg was a terrible old lady called Mary Midnight.

Mrs Midnight, witch and midwife, was a woman of ageless experience limited only by arrested development. She listened in regularly to the councils of European courts and gave inside information about them, with a pitying word now and again for "my good sister Benedict XIV" whose state had fallen so low since "holy Mother Joan sat upon the Sacred See." She was an honorary member of the Royal Society and the Society of Antiquarians, and kept on the alert for curious discoveries in all parts of the country, such as "the *bona fide* petrified Excrement . . . a Monument of ancient Simplicity" which she reported from the county of Cornwall. She patrolled the seamier districts of London with an eye especially for the misfortunes of young women and the consumption of gin. She built up a large body of correspondents, both animal and human, to whom she replied punctiliously; especially concerning marriage, a subject on which she was peculiarly qualified by her profession to give advice: "such is the Opinion of *Solomon*, such of *Socrates*, such of *Sir Thomas More*, and such of *Mary Midnight*, four persons to which all the Ages in the World shall never be able to add a fifth." She could even peer into the future and describe the state of England in the year, say, 1931.

By exploring these and other avenues she managed to fill about fifty octavo pages every month with an exotic hotch-potch of nonsensical titbits, scholastic, topical, medical,

53

philosophical, the whole flavoured with a very pungent earthy seasoning and stirred with unfailing flippancy and zest: price threepence, at J. Newbery's, the *Bible and Sun*, in St Paul's Churchyard. According to Hunter's memoir, the entire composition of *The Midwife* was in the hands of Smart and Newbery. Smart himself did nearly all the actual writing, perhaps with occasional help from Rolt or Thornton or Murphy. Every number, however, reprinted a story or essay from *The Rambler* by arrangement with Johnson. It is interesting to mark the underlying seriousness of Johnson in contrast with the determined triviality of Smart.

The humour of *The Midwife* was admirably and variously maintained for more than two years, but after a while the modern reader begins to be appalled by its deliberately ephemeral juvenility: never once the keen bite of intellectual satire, never the thrill of creative fantasy that can play on different levels, no sign that the author is a poet. Johnson launched his *Rambler* with a private prayer of great devotion; Smart launched his *Midwife* with a public preface which seemed carefree enough, but we who have followed his career from infancy as closely as possible can tell that it was a private act of betrayal; for the "Good-Nature" he dismisses with such apparent ease in the extract here quoted was the name that he gave to his dearest possession, his poetic muse.

Wisdom is a substantial Being, *Wit* an imaginary one, and between these two was begot *Humour*, who is a sort of HERM-APHRODITE and neither real nor imaginary. Wisdom was always greatly enamoured of *Truth*, because she was naked, and between them was begot *Good-Nature*; but she long since died of a Hectic under the Hands of Dr. —— So that the only Beings now that preside over Poets (except the Muses, who by the way are become mere Prostitutes) are *Wisdom*, *Wit*, and *Humour*; who seat themselves in the Brain, and there make as much Bustle, as *Pride*, *Love*, and *Reason* did in the breast of the Princess . . .

> Pride, Love and Reason fight till ye are cloyed,
> And each by each in mutual Wounds destroyed.
> Thus when a Barber and a Collier fight,
> The Barber beats the luckless Collier—white!
> The dusty Collier heaves his ponderous Sack
> And, big with vengeance, beats the Barber—black!

> In comes the Brick-dust Man, with Grime o'erspread,
> And beats the Collier and the Barber—red!
> Black, red, and white, in various Clouds are tossed,
> And in the Dust they raise, the Combatants are lost.

Just so did Smart blur the edges of his sensitivity. The dark evils of eighteenth-century London, the sorrows of humanity in general, the irony and comedy in human institutions, all make frequent appearances in *The Midwife*, but all are smothered equally by the remorseless blanket of burlesque. There have been various guesses about the origin of the name, Mother Midnight; I should think that, partially at any rate, it was suggested to Smart by the last two lines of the *Dunciad*:

> Thy hand, great Anarch, lets the curtain fall;
> And universal Darkness buries All.

As might be expected, a succession of new features was necessary to keep *The Midwife* going, and, again as might be expected, very little of Smart's personal opinions are allowed to seep through. One feature of 1751 has a certain gruesome interest; it was a series of visits paid by Mrs Midnight to Bethlehem or Bedlam, the public madhouse in Moorfields. The general opinion, borne out by Hogarth's picture, was that religious mania and frustrated love were the two chief agents in filling Bedlam. Mrs Midnight, however, discovered from a friend that the place was full of politicians:

"Why, a Doctor of my Acquaintance, who keeps a private House of Entertainment for these Sorts of People, was showing me t'other day his Patients, which he had classed according to their different disorders . . . *viz.*, Love of POWER, Love of FAME, Love of WEALTH, and that other sort of Love which you and I were acquainted with in our younger Days. . . . The mad Men of the three former Class, Madam, are so considerable, that the latter bears no proportion with them; and then they are abundantly the most obstinate and incorrigible. . . . Some were such Bigots that they would take no Medicines nor eat any Thing but what had the letters *G.R.* upon it; nor would the other suffer any Thing to be brought near them but what was embellished with the characters *J.R.*"

Smart's mild aversion from all politics may have concealed a sneaking and unavowed sympathy with Jacobitism. It is worth noting that he shows no sign at all of that fixed and

55

bitter hatred of Rome which was a marked feature of his later life—only a genial contempt, quite free from malice, as in this conversation jotted down at a gin shop by Mrs Midnight, a recollection of 1745:

CRIB: I tell you, Master Patch, 'tis this War, 'tis this d'mned War that makes every thing so plaguy dear.

PATCH: Are we at war now with the *Turks* or *Infidels*?

CRIB: No, no—'tis with the *French*, and the Queen of *Hung-a-ry*.

JERRY: Aye, aye—'tis with the *Papishes*, 'tis with the *Papishes*.

PATCH: Are those *Papishes* the great *Hottentots* that eat Men?

CRIB: Pshaw! you Fool,—your *Papish* is a Man as you or I may be. He wont eat a Morsel of you, if he was ready to starve.

JERRY: But he will broil you upon a Gridiron tho', if you dont believe in the Pope and the Devil, and kiss the Pretender's great Toe.

PATCH: Who may that same Pretender be? Can you give a Body a Subscription of him?

CRIB: Why, as to that there—your Pretender is your Fellow that pretends to this and that and t'other, in the Way of Talk;—and after all his pretending, 'tis an errant Pretence—that there is your Pretender.

PATCH: To be certain, its a rare thing to be a Scolard.

Perhaps one more example may be allowed of Smart's typical and traditional humour. Mr Justice Bundle addresses the Grand Jury:

All Laws are Laws, and every Law is a Law, and Laws are things made by the Lawyers to make Men live according to Law, without any respect to the Gospel, for that is another affair, and to be considered at another Opportunity, and by another Sort of Men, and in another Manner. *Vide Coke upon Littleton*, Chap. X, Page 15, But as to the Law—Now there are some Men that are good Men, and some Men that are bad Men, and the bad Men are not the good Men, and the good Men are not the bad Men. But the bad Men and the good Men, and the good Men and the bad Men are two different sorts of Men, and this we gather from *Magna Charta*, an old Man that lived in the reign of King John the Great. Now if all Men were good Men there would be no need of Law; therefore, *Ergo*, the Laws were made for the bad Men, and the good Men have no Business therewith, nor no advantage to receive therefrom. *Ergo*, therefore, those that receive advantage from the Law must be bad Men. And so, Gentlemen, call up the Prisoners, and despatch them as soon as possible, for I must go out of Town tomorrow.

This book is a life of Smart, not a monograph on eighteenth-century journalism, so we now say goodbye to Mrs Midnight—except so far as she indicates the events in Smart's life.

January 1751 marked the outbreak of one of those literary street-fights in which this period abounded. An amiable guttersnipe called Kenrick, who considered that anything approaching scurrility was his exclusive province, became jealous of Mrs Midnight's popularity. He and Smart clashed in a public tournament. But Smart was new to this sort of street warfare. He proclaimed in one issue of *The Midwife* that the next would contain a complete pulverization of Kenrick. The pulverization appeared somewhat prematurely, bearing all the outward marks of being by Smart, but actually written by Kenrick and redounding to Smart's discredit. His indignant proof in the next issue that his style had been counterfeited came rather as an anticlimax.

In March 1751, in reaction from this low company, it was with great relief that Smart became involved once more with his aristocratic friends, the Delavals. There was a rage for amateur theatricals. The Delaval family and their friends decided to put on a play. A play by Will Shakespeare. *Othello*! What choice could be more suitable? And who more suitable to help and guide the production than their old friend Kit Smart? One of the Delavals played Othello and the other Iago. It took place at Drury Lane Theatre and the Prince and Princess of Wales were present amid "the most brilliant audience that perhaps ever was assembled upon any Occasion," commented Mrs Midnight. "The whole Performance was truly admirable, and merited all the Applause that was or could be given it." It must have been a riot—not the least successful part being Smart's epilogue, spoken by a pert and dishevelled Desdemona, beginning:

> True Woman to the last—my *peroration*
> I come to speak in spight of Suffocation;
> To show the present and the Age to come
> We may be choak'd, but never can be dumb.

As a result of this triumph, Smart's interest in the theatre sharpened. Mrs Midnight tried her hand at both dramatic and artistic criticism. Garrick and Hogarth, it is clear, were now among Smart's friends. But at the same time he was receiving some sharp criticism from *The Gentleman's Magazine* for wasting his talent.

57

A less happy result of his new theatrical interest was a stunt conceived by Newbery and himself to whip up the circulation of *The Midwife*. In the winter of 1751 Mrs. Midnight was billed to appear in person with a supporting cast at the Castle Tavern in Paternoster Row. The show took its title from a well-known comic feature of London life who had recently passed away—"Orator" Henley, a crazy tub-thumping atheist who used to escape arrest for blasphemy because of his entertainment value. Smart's show was called "The Old Woman's Oratory" or "Henley in Petticoats"; he probably played Mrs. Midnight and possibly other parts as well. It was music-hall entertainment, songs, dances, farces, etc., later helped out by a troupe of performing animals. Its success was such that in December 1751 it moved to the New Theatre in the Haymarket. Beginning as an advertisement for *The Midwife* it ended by taking its place. Smart became so involved in the show that the written magazine petered out in 1752 and made only one sporadic appearance in 1753. He felt, probably, that if he was to make a fool of himself, he might as well go the whole hog; he would be relieved, anyway, to have a change from the monthly drudgery of fifty pages of forced humour.

His reputation as a serious writer might by now have been sorely imperilled had he not made strenuous and industrious efforts to maintain it. The Prince of Wales had died, shortly after his visit to *Othello*, and Smart composed a *Dirge* which won him much commendation, though it is insipid to modern taste; it was successfully performed to music by Worgan at the Vauxhall Gardens where the Prince had been an *habitué*. Then in April of the same year he again won the Seatonian prize; some lines of this 1751 poem were quoted on page 12. Meanwhile he was working away at the delayed edition of his collected poems which Newbery had promised to publish. It appeared eventually in June 1752 under the title *Poems on Several Occasions* and must be reckoned a genuine and unqualified success. Beautifully produced by Thomas Carnan (Newbery's stepson and printer), it had a list of more than seven hundred subscribers which guaranteed a handsome net profit. Among them, apart from all Smart's friends already mentioned, were such famous names as "Mr. Voltaire, historiographer of France," Roubillac the sculptor (a distant connection of Smart), and Richardson the novelist; it is interesting to note also the names of Thomas Gray and his friend Mason, whose gloomy predictions about Smart seemed well on the way to being falsified. It must be remembered that Smart had become a hack writer simply as a means to the end of getting his poems published and making his name known. Now that this object was triumphantly accomplished he seems to have made a determined effort to settle down as a writer on a higher plane.

He was already practically free from *The Midwife*, and the arrival of the troupe of performing animals in the winter of 1752 set him free also from *Henley in Petticoats*. He was thus able to concentrate, and on November 2 was awarded the Seatonian Prize for the third successive year; his poem on this occasion, the least interesting and spontaneous of his five winners, was dedicated to the Archbishop of Canterbury. He now determined to cut free from the literary underworld of London with one resounding and self-justifying blow.

The occasion was the great paper war of 1752-3 in which Henry Fielding had become involved and was suffering from a variety of attacks by Kenrick and others. Fielding, whom Smart much admired, was reckoned to be the champion of literary genius against mediocre dullness. Smart and his friend Murphy decided to come to his rescue with a satire against the underworld which would establish Smart as the poet who had the best right to be considered Pope's successor. This time Kenrick was carefully avoided and a much more vulnerable victim selected. This was a certain "Sir" John Hill. A botanist of real talent (he had a plant named after him, *Hillia parasitica*), he had made a lot of money by popular works of science, but nourished a morbid desire to be a literary pundit as well as a man of fashion. His indestructible vanity and the low state of English letters enabled him to be successful for a while, in spite of some severe setbacks; on one occasion an Irish writer, whose spelling he had ridiculed in his paper, carried the dispute to a different level by beating Hill in public with a cane.

This was the man, a particular enemy of Fielding, against whom Smart and Murphy planned and executed *The Hilliad* in imitation of Pope's *Dunciad*. Smart wrote it extempore, striding up and down the room, with Murphy goading him on and adding long and facetious footnotes. Newbery published it early in 1753, along with two introductory letters. It achieved its purpose of demolishing Hill, temporarily at any rate, but I can find only two lines in it remotely worthy of Pope; this was the couplet used the following year in cartoons against Hill when he attacked Fielding once more over the famous Elizabethan Canning case:

> The checquer'd world's before thee—go—farewell,
> Beware of Irishmen—and learn to spell.

More interesting to a biographer are the introductory letters—evidence of Smart's desire to prove that he had entered Grub Street only in order to teach it a lesson. The first is to a poet friend at Cambridge, where Smart had been taking a holiday to write his Seatonian prize poem. From the description, the friend sounds just like Thomas Gray; at any rate it is one poet of genius talking to another in detached and rarefied terms:

> The design and colouring of a poem, such as you have planned, are not to be executed in a hurry, but with slow and careful touches, which will give that finishing to your piece, remarkable in everything that comes from your hand, and which I could wish the precipitancy of my temper would permit me to aim at upon all occasions.

Smart goes on to describe the deplorable state of literary criticism in the metropolis. Casually he mentions the attacks on his poor friend Fielding by this extraordinary creature Hill, who "will not hesitate, in order to make himself talked of at any rate, to become most glaringly ridiculous. This [adds Smart with revolting smugness, considering Mrs Midnight] answers the purpose of the booksellers as well perhaps as Attick wit, and hence it results that they are willing to continue him in their pay." As an afterthought, he asks the Cambridge poet's advice about publishing the enclosed trifle, *The Hilliad*.

Whether or not this letter was meant to seem to be

addressed to Gray, there is no doubt that it was Arthur Murphy who wrote the second letter, the answer. It urges on Smart his clear moral duty to demolish Hill and restore the republic of letters to its pristine honour, and it warmly commends him as the rightful successor to Pope in the war against dullness.

With the publication of *The Hilliad* Smart concluded three years of frantic industry and breathtaking versatility. He seemed to have reached a point, however precarious, where he could pause for a while and bask in the sun.

During these years he had changed his address—a change whose implications demand a fresh chapter. He had moved from his lodging near St James's Park, Westminister, to Canbury (or Canonbury), to an old house in Islington rented by Mr Newbery. Some time in 1752 Smart had married a girl with golden locks called Nancy Carnan. She was Mr Newbery's step-daughter.

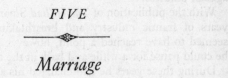

FIVE

Marriage

JOHN NEWBERY was born in 1713 in the village of Waltham St Lawrence in Berkshire, where his name was a well-known one; his ancestor, Ralf Newberie, Master of the Stationers' Company in the reign of Queen Elizabeth, had left his estate in trust to help "the poorest and neediest" of his native parish. Ralf's descendants in the next century were content to be modest farmers until John, a younger son, went off to Reading Town with his father's blessing in 1730 to seek his fortune and repeat the bookselling triumphs of his ancestor.

At sixteen he was apprenticed to William Carnan, owner and printer of the *Reading Mercury*, one of the earliest provincial newspapers. He served his master so well that when Carnan came to die in 1737 he left half the business to John Newbery. In 1740 Newbery married the widow, Mary Carnan, and acquired the business outright. Then in 1744 he came up to London with his wife and children to expand his fortunes still further. He had three little children by Mrs. Newbery in her second marriage, and there were three step-children from the first: John Carnan who stayed in Reading to print the *Mercury*, Thomas who became Newbery's printer in London, and Anna-Maria (Nancy).

Mrs Newbery was the daughter of Martin Hounshill, a brazier of Ringwood, of old Hampshire recusant stock; her brother, also a Martin, was ordained priest in 1742. In Reading Mrs Carnan (now Newbery) and her daughter had gone to Mass at the private chapel of Mapledurham where

Pope's friend, Martha Blount, lived. In London, though her name occurs in the registers of the Lincoln's Inn Fields Chapel, she would probably have gone to the crowded Mass-centre of St Mary Moorfields in Ropemakers Alley; but unfortunately all the early records of this chapel were destroyed in the Gordon riots of 1780.

According to the custom prevalent at that time in marriages of mixed religion, the boys were brought up in their father's persuasion, the girls in their mother's. Thus Thomas and John Carnan were Protestants, Anna-Maria was a Catholic. Newbery seems to have followed the same custom; his little daughter Mary, born about 1742, was evidently brought up like her mother, for she later married a Catholic wine-merchant, Michael Power. Newbery was a good husband and a good father; he did not let religious differences cloud his family relations; in his will of 1762 he left money to his brother-in-law Martin, the priest, as well as to his Hounshill sisters-in-law. Under his sturdy protection his wife and step-daughter were safe in the discreet practice of their proscribed religion.

Smart was brought onto more intimate terms with the Newbery-Carnan household by a sad event in 1751; the death of the eldest child of the second marriage, after a lingering illness bravely borne. Smart wrote some very dignified and sensitive lines on the subject, ending:

> His painful Race undauntedly he ran,
> And on the eleventh Winter died a MAN.

Anna-Maria was nineteen years old when Smart was introduced to her. The story of their courtship is told in half a dozen love songs. His first impression was one of awe at her "adamantine Innocence." But before the end of the year he was proclaiming to the world that there was no one to rival Nancy:

> No more of my Harriot, of Polly no more,
> Nor all the bright beauties that charm'd me before;
> My heart for a slave to gay Venus I've sold,
> And barter'd my freedom for ringlets of gold:
> I'll throw down my pipe, and neglect all my flocks,
> And will sing to my lass with the golden locks. . ..

63

Than the swan in the brook she's more dear to my sight,
Her mien is more stately, her breast is more white,
Her lips are like rubies, all rubies above,
Which are fit for the language and labour of love;
At the park in the mall, at the play in the box,
My lass bears the bell with her golden locks.

And for her birthday on 26 January 1752, after some more
rhapsodizing:

Let but those Lips their Sweets disclose,
    And rich Perfumes exhale,
We shall not want the fragrant Rose
    Nor miss the southern Gale.
Then loosely to the Winds unfold,
Those radiant Locks of burnish'd Gold.

he introduced a more practical note:

This Day each warmest Wish be paid
    To thee the Muse's Pride,
I long to see the blooming Maid
    Chang'd to the blushing Bride.

The matter seems to have been settled when Smart fell
seriously ill with fever and was nursed back to health by
Miss Carnan. He was then presumably staying at Canonbury
House in Islington where Newbery had rented apartments.
In a poem to a pet bird, which Miss Carnan had also nursed
back to health, he concluded soberly:

Me too the kind indulgent maid
With gen'rous care and timely aid
    Restor'd to mirth and health;
Then join'd to her, O may I prove
By friendship, gratitude and love
    The poverty of wealth.

On 3 May 1753 their first child was born, Marianne, called
after Smart's younger sister; this is the "Polly" of Smart's
later endearments whom over-eager commentators have
identified with a "former sweetheart." On 27 October of the
following year came their second daughter, Elizabeth Anne
("Bess") to whom we owe various slight but valuable bits of
information about her father.

On 26 January 1754 Smart was still very much in love with his wife:

> 'Tis *Nancy's* birth-day—raise your strains,
> Ye nymphs of the Parnassian plains,
> And sing with more than usual glee
> To *Nancy* who was born for me. . . .
>
> Tell royal *Venus*, though she rove,
> The queen of the immortal grove;
> That she must share her golden fee
> With *Nancy*, who was born for me . . .
>
> Tell spotless *Dian*, though she range,
> The regent of the up-land grange,
> In chastity she yields to thee,
> O, *Nancy*, who wast born for me.

And the second anniversary of their wedding was still for him:

> That day, when to my longing arms,
> Nancy resign'd her golden charms.

Nevertheless a certain mystery still surrounds the exact time and place of the event. It is generally assigned to the year 1753; but Mrs Smart, in the dates she gave to her daughters, is quite definite that it took place in 1752. There is every reason to believe her. It was naturally kept secret as long as possible so that Smart could go on getting the money from his Fellowship.

The wedding, therefore, was before the Hardwicke Act of 1753 which obliged marriages to be registered by an Anglican clergyman. All the same one would expect there to be some record of it. But none has been found—not in the parish church of Islington, nor in the surviving registers of any nearby church or chapel, nor among the special licences. More surprising perhaps, there is no record of the baptism of the elder child Marianne. On the other hand, the baptism of the younger, Elizabeth, is registered in the Islington parish church, St Mary's Canonbury, on 25 November 1754.

The Durham historian Surtees, in his short biography of Smart, incorporated some interesting information about the courtship and marriage from the younger daughter Elizabeth, who presumably had it from her mother or her aunt.

The story, in what appears to be Elizabeth's own words, is as follows:

> The family were residing at Canonbury House, Islington, where Smart was a constant visitor. An intimacy, which soon ripened into affection, took place between him and Anna-Maria Carnan, daughter of Mrs. Newbery by her first Husband. A clandestine marriage took place, without the consent of Mr. Newbery, whose favour however was soon conciliated, and Smart was immediately established at Canonbury House, where he pursued his literary labours for several years. A gleam of steady light seemed now opening on his prospects, and nothing, I think, has been alleged against his domestic habits.[1]

By a "clandestine marriage" cannot be meant one of those disreputable ones performed by the unfrocked "Bishop" Keith in the Fleet chapel or in Mayfair; for even these were recorded (on the day before the Hardwicke Act came into force, the "Bishop" rushed through 217 couples, working—Horace Walpole tells us—from 8 a.m. to 8 p.m. "Happy is the wooing, that is not long a-doing" was his motto); in any case Anna-Maria would never have consented, nor Newbery ever have been reconciled, to such a wedding. It seems likely, though it is only an argument from silence, that the clandestine marriage was a Catholic one. By the same argument of silence, Marianne would have been baptized in the chapel of St Mary Moorfields—the centre for Islington Catholics—whose records, like those of some other Catholic chapels were destroyed in the Gordon riots.[2]

This would mean that Smart, following Newbery's example, allowed his elder daughter, Polly, to be baptized in the religion of her mother and her grandmother; but that when it came to the second daughter, he insisted on the Church of England. The matter is not one of just getting the records straight. The truth is that Smart's attitude to his

[1] Surtees, *History . . . of Durham*, IV, p. 143, published in 1840 but written in 1832 when Elizabeth (Mrs Le Noir) was alive and still, aged 78, conducting with her niece a school for young ladies at Caversham Priory, Reading. Her information was conveyed in a letter to Sir C. Sharp. I do not know if the original is still in existence.

[2] The Boulogne Ursuline convent, where Marianne and Elizabeth were educated, would have provided evidence of Marianne's baptism, but unfortunately all its records were burnt to ashes in the Second World War. The Reading Mission box, in the Portsmouth archives, perished by the same agency.

wife and to her religion is an important clue to his later madness. One of the obsessions of his religious mania was that he had married "a Moabitish woman" and that his elder child had been alienated from "the house of David"; this was part of the larger obsession that he was a sort of prophet, or even a messiah, through whom the Church of England was destined to become Catholic and Universal.

If the marriage were a Catholic one and Polly (though not Bess) baptized a Catholic, it would explain several passages in the madhouse document *Jubilate Agno*, whose significance has hitherto been missed. For example, invoking the blessings of Naomi and Ruth, he has these two versicles, written in 1759, during the Seven Years War:

> Let Naomi rejoice. . . . For I pray God to bless POLLY in the blessing of Naomi and assign her to the house of David.
>
> Let Ruth rejoice. . . . For I am in charity with the French who are my foes and Moabites because of the Moabitish woman.

The editors' comment is: "*Polly* is unidentified, but was mentioned by Smart as a former sweetheart in 'The Lass with the Golden Locks'." But Polly here is Marianne. Smart is praying that she may be brought up in "the house of David," that is, the Church of England, in spite of her being baptized "a Moabite"—the traditional puritan name for Roman Catholic. In the second versicle he is taking comfort from the example of Ruth, ancestress of David and of Our Saviour, who was a Moabitess like his wife: but he is dismayed none the less at having to be in charity with the French who are Moabites.

It is very important to note that there is no trace of these crazy sectarian notions in the years that immediately followed his marriage. On the contrary, all the evidence is of broad tolerance and domestic content.

As for young Mrs Smart, she was such a silent and self-effacing person that it is hard to say anything about her. But by subtraction from Smart's early hyperboles, and by addition or inference from later facts, one can compile at least a list of adjectives. She was quiet, graceful, capable, tactful, shrewd, well-read, kind-hearted and pious. It may be also that she was implacable. We do not know. What we do know is that from thirty to eighty she practised her proscribed religion and ran a successful business (the *Reading Mercury*) without forfeiting the respect of anyone who knew her. Her stepfather, Newbery, was devoted to her, and so were her sisters-in-law, Smart's sisters; Dr Johnson admired her deeply; her daughters worshipped her. She was not a woman whose influence on Smart's life can be dismissed with a shrug either of pity or of contempt.

He was pretty well off for money in 1753. So from now on he took a well-earned rest from journalism, and he renounced altogether the rowdy warfare that was inseparable from journalism. When the paper battle around Henry Fielding flared up again in 1754 over the Elizabeth Canning case, Smart took no part in it. He was busy with a collection of "Fables" in verse, eighteen in all. One or two had appeared in his collected poems, and three or four were published in the *Gentleman's Magazine*; but most of them remained with his family awaiting a new collection of his poems. Although modelled on Gay's *Fables* and professing the same intentions:

> Bigots, avaunt, sense can't endure ye,
> But fabulists should try to cure ye.

they lack Gay's sharp-drawn, witty moral, and are rather fanciful and vaguely thoughtful, relapsing into levity when the author seems unable to find the courage, or at least the clarity of his convictions. Nevertheless, most of them are a pleasant contrast with the strident buffoonery of *The Midwife*, and they are interesting biographically as showing how far from Smart's mind at that time was any kind of crazy religious nationalism. Two of the fables may be taken as examples.

A Story of a Cock and Bull is an indictment of contemporary cruelty to animals; but it opens with a laugh against excessively complacent patriotism:

> The land of liberty we tread,
> And woe to his devoted head,
> Who dares the contrary advance,
> One Englishman's worth ten of France.

> These these, are truths, what man won't write for
> Won't swear, won't bully, or won't fight for,
> Yet (tho' perhaps I speak thro' vanity)
> Wou'd we'd a little more humanity;
> Too far, I fear, I've drove the jest,
> So leave to cock and bull the rest.

There follows the story about an old worn-out bull who is cruelly sent to the village to be baited. Smart introduces him with one of his irrepressible cackles:

> A bull, who'd listen'd to the vows
> Of above fifteen hundred cows;

But there is a genuine pathos in the story as it proceeds:

> Victorious yet the bull return'd,
> And with stern silence inly mourn'd.

and in the gallant old cock who has suffered similar wrongs and who cheers the bull with these words:

> Methinks at every dawn of day
> When first I chant my blithsome lay,
> Methinks I hear from out the sky,
> All will be better by and by;
> When bloody, base, degenerate man,
> Who deviates from his Maker's plan;
> Who Nature and her works abuses
> And thus his fellow servants uses,
> Shall greatly, and yet justly want,
> The mercy he refus'd to grant;
> And (while his heart his conscience purges)
> Shall wish to be the brute he scourges.

The other fable, *The English Bull Dog, Dutch Mastiff, and Quail*, follows the same line, but here the protest against cruelty to animals is incidental, the main theme is:

> Are we not all of race divine,
> Alike of an immortal line? . . .
> Souls, sprung from an etherial flame,
> However clad, are still the same. . . .
> Dame Nature, who, all meritorious,
> In a true Englishman is glorious;
> Is lively, honest, brave and bonny,
> In Monsieur, Taffy, Teague and Sawney.
> Give prejudices to the wind,
> And let's be patriots of mankind.

After the English and Dutch dogs have made ludicrous claims each for its own breed or nation, the captive quail rebukes them:

> 'Wrong are you both,' rejoins a quail,
> Confin'd within its wiry jail:
> 'Frequent from realm to realm I've rang'd
> And with the seasons, climates chang'd.
> Mankind is not so void of grace,
> But good I've found in every place:
> I've seen sincerity in France,
> Amongst the Germans complaisance;
> In foggy Holland wit may reign,
> I've known humility in Spain;
> Free'd was I by a turban'd Turk
> Whose life was one entire good work;
> And in this land, fair freedom's boast,
> Behold, my liberty is lost.
> Despis'd Hibernia have I seen
> Dejected like a widow'd queen.'

The rest of the fable is concerned with the woes of Ireland and the hopes placed on Lord Hartington's Lord-Lieutenancy. This fixes the date of composition as April 1755, and it also reminds us that about this time Smart's sister, Marianne, had married an Irish barrister, Richard Falkiner of Mount Falcon, Tipperary, and gone to live there. The other sister, Margaret, married Dr Hunter, a surgeon of Margate. They were probably both now better off than their brother.

These pleasant and civilized fables and other short poems published in the *Gentleman's Magazine* were hardly enough to keep Smart and his little family in funds. By 1755 he had almost certainly run through the capital acquired from his collected poems and other works. Moreover, in the previous year he had apparently again been seriously ill, perhaps with the same kind of fever as in 1752; but this time it prevented him from competing for the Seatonian prize and for the first time in five years it went elsewhere.

This was the time, with his wife occupied with two babies, that shadows may have begun to fall on the household. "He was so thoughtless," Hunter feels bound to record, "that he has often, as his widow relates, invited company to dinner when no means appeared of providing a meal for themselves."

70

Money troubles and unhappiness at home often lead to getting drunk away from home; and here I think should be considered the evidence about Smart's drunkenness.

The Missouri authors of his life, Professors Ainsworth and Noyes, present a very black picture of a home that "could hardly have been anything but drab and unhappy . . . darkened by debt, poverty, drunkenness, and—later—insanity as well." But this seems to me a view darkened not by the evidence so much as by the general gloom that descends upon harassed research students. The account that claims to have his daughter's authority says of these years that "a gleam of steady light seemed now opening on his prospects, and nothing, I think, has been alleged against his domestic habits." Hunter, it is true, says that his uncle's "chief fault" was "deviation from the rules of sobriety"; but Hunter may only have been voicing strict clerical disapproval of strong drink in any degree or form. The degree or form, however, matters a great deal; strong drink is not necessarily a mortal threat to the happiness of married life. I think the evidence, such as it is, suggests that Smart was a light-hearted drinker who succumbed with fatal ease in convivial company; that he was not a confirmed or vicious drunkard; and that for long periods he was free from the evil altogether.

We know that he drank too much at Cambridge about 1746, but he seems to have pulled himself together after the occasion when he was nearly arrested for debt. In his first three years in London, 1750–2, his literary output was so enormous that he could not possibly have been a confirmed drunkard. The only evidence against him at that time comes from the hardened old toper Kenrick in his Pasquinade of January 1753, but he seems to be mocking Smart not for heavy drinking but for being unable to hold his drink—a fatal handicap in the eighteenth century—"See him," says Kenrick—

> With Cyder muddled, or inspired with Bub,
> In Newbery's Garret, or in Henley's Tub,
> With Coachmen, Coblers, and such dainty folks,
> For Mugs of Porter pun and crack his jokes.

For the later years the evidence comes from his friend Dr Johnson, and it does sound rather damning. "He used, before his confinement, to walk to the ale-house for exercise," Johnson is reported as saying, "but he was *carried* back." But about this conversation we need Mrs Thrale as our guide, not Boswell. Mrs Thrale quotes it as an example of Johnson's humorous perversity; he would take up some impossible position—in this case, that no man needed to take any exercise—and then say the first outrageous thing that came into his head to support it.

It is quite likely, however, that Smart struck a bad patch in the latter half of 1754 or the beginning of 1755. But, if so, he pulled himself together again; for, as will be seen in a moment, he was very hard at work during most of that year making money for himself and his family.

On the whole then I think Smart was probably justified in looking back wistfully to Canonbury House as a place of happiness: "For I bless God for my retreat at Canbury, as it was the place of the nativity of my children." His daughter, too, had pleasant reminiscences of the place:

> Ah, still in fancy's eyes are seen
> The stately elms that formed its screen;
> Where my good grandsire, loved, caressed,
> Watched the old magpye build her nest,
> Or marked in distance just descried
> The small white vessels smoothly glide,
> As hills, half-veiled in aether blue,
> Pointed old Thames's course to view.[1]

They do not go, of course, back as far as 1755, when she was only a year old. But one of her stories does, a story of how on at least *one* occasion her father was not "carried back" from the ale-house, but returned with a tale that made her mother laugh and recollect it to tell her daughters in later years:

I well remember the high trees that screened the back of the dwelling, and the very old house they partly concealed, the habitation of the justice of the peace whose name was Booth: the out-door guard was a large, lean mastiff, in very ill condition, whose howlings were a great annoyance to the neighbours. One morning Mr. Smart going as usual to read the newspapers at the Public house, meeting there with Justice Booth, was accosted by him with, "So, Mr. Smart, the dog's

[1] Elizabeth Smart Le Noir, *Miscellaneous Poems*, 1826. The good grandsire was John Newbery.

dead." "I am glad of it," he replied. "Why so, Mr. Smart?" "Why, because he was half starved and always howling: I had thought of being at the expense of a brace of pistols myself, to put him out of his misery." "Pooh, pooh," exclaimed the Justice, "not my dog—I mean the Dog of Venice!"

In 1755 Smart was working hard at a task which was very galling and distasteful to him, but lucrative. It was a translation in prose for Newbery of the complete work of Horace. Smart loved Horace deeply and longed to translate him into verse; but this was a rush job, done purely for money. In that it succeeded; it went through several editions and became a famous crib; though its Bohns have now disintegrated, it is still read by schoolboys, and Smart's name still survives in the Everyman translation. Smart got £100 for it from Newbery. He complained later that he personally saw only £13 of this; the rest was advanced to his family. Newbery was a benevolent patriarch; the money was probably spent much more wisely than it would have been by Smart; but Smart no doubt felt that Newbery was usurping his position as head of the house.

This may have been the beginning of a rift with Newbery. But, if so, it was not yet on Newbery's side. He was very anxious to go on printing and publishing for Smart. Several times that winter he advertised the forthcoming appearance of the *Fables* in verse, and seems to have been only waiting for a few more to finish the collection. He also wanted to publish the collected Seatonian poems. Smart, girding himself for the fray, had rushed in and carried off the 1755 award, finishing his manuscript in October, only just in time. It was dedicated to his old patron, Lord Barnard, who had recently been made Earl of Darlington.

Smart's religious opinions at this time, so far as they can be assessed, were old-fashioned "Anglo-Catholic." He sympathized with Atterbury and disliked Warburton. The divine who most nearly represented his views, though there is no evidence of any contact between them, would have been William Law. There is no evidence that Smart knew Law, but an examination of the *Song to David* (see Chapter Eleven) shows a deep and inward similarity in their Christological tenets. As regards externals, Smart held by mysteries and miracles, prayers for the dead, devotion to the angels and saints,[1] especially the Blessed Virgin Mary whose divine motherhood he strongly upheld.

> When from the Virgin's unpolluted womb,
> Shone forth the Sun of Righteousness reveal'd.

His feeling for the accidentals of ritual orthodoxy—incense, chant and stained-glass windows—is brought out in this passage which may be quoted, incidentally, as an example of the facility of his religious expression. It continues from the passage about the song of birds quoted on page 12:

> But not to all,—for hark, the organs blow
> Their swelling notes round the cathedral's dome,
> And grace th' harmonious choir, celestial feast
> To pious ears, and med'cine of the mind;
> The thrilling trebles and the manly base
> Join in accordance meet, and with one voice
> All to the sacred subject suit their song:
> While in each breast sweet melancholy reigns
> Angelically pensive, till the joy
> Improves and purifies;—the solemn scene
> The Sun through storied panes surveys with awe,
> And bashfully with-holds each bolder beam.
> Here, as her home, from morn to eve frequents
> The cherub Gratitude;—behold her eyes!
> With love and gladness weepingly they shed
> Ecstatic smiles; the incense, that her hands
> Uprear, is sweeter than the breath of May
> Caught from the nectarine's blossom, and her voice
> Is more than voice can tell; to him she sings,
> To him who feeds, who clothes and who adorns,
> Who made and who preserves, whatever dwells
> In air, in steadfast earth, or fickle sea—
> O he is good, he is immensely good!

It was probably towards the end of 1755 that there occurred the strange incident with Lord Darlington, his patron, which Hunter records as an example of his uncle's "shyness":

[1] Though Smart was later accused of "offering prayers to the dead," and though he sometimes gives the impression that the saints and angels, especially the angels, are interceding for us, he probably never meant to exceed the classical Anglican position of honouring them.

Having undertaken to introduce his wife to my Lord Darlington, with whom he was well acquainted; he had no sooner mentioned her name to his Lordship, than he retreated suddenly, as if stricken with panic, from the room, and from the house, leaving her to follow overwhelmed with confusion.

Mr Brittain, who has it in for Anna-Maria, comments: "The Carnans and the Newberys were not the sort of people who could get out of such a situation gracefully." Nor, apparently, was the Earl of Darlington.

It seems to be a situation that needs more than shyness to explain it. It looks like a premonition of those irrational outbursts of nervous anger and distress which began to divorce Smart from his "normal" sweet and friendly self. Rationalized, perhaps it would have found some such words as, "I am a chosen soul. By this time I should have been moving at ease among the great ones of this world, consulted and revered, instead of being checked continually by Newbery's pettifogging exactitude and my wife's demands for money."

Smart was much too decent a fellow to give conscious and deliberate expression to such sentiments. He did, however, after completing the prose Horace, make a sharp effort to break away from Newbery's purse-strings. Along with his friend and hanger-on, Richard Rolt (not a reliable person), he entered on a gradiose contract with Gardener the bookseller and Allen the printer. They were to launch a sixpenny general-knowledge magazine called *The Universal Visitor*; Smart and Rolt were to share one-third of the gross takings, and they contracted not to write for any other periodical—this did not include books, pamphlets, etc.—for the legal term of ninety-nine years.

But by the time the first number appeared, in February 1756, Smart was struck down by an attack of fever, the third and most dangerous since he came to London. This illness was the prelude to a completely new phase in his life.

SIX

Madness

IN narrating the events of Smart's life in the year 1756, one is conscious both of a great glory and of a great sadness. There is a great glory in the way he rises from his sick-bed a completely new man, mind and heart wholly intent upon his Maker and Redeemer; there is glory in the way he sets about immediately, like a busy workman, to pound and shape the golden language of Spenser till it glows and vibrates with quite a new power of God-directed thought and feeling. It is laborious work at first; but here at last, after much fumbling, is the man who will write *A Song to David*; you notice already the hammering that joins stanza to stanza— "feet," "eyes," "nerves"—in these lines, so different from the slipshod facility of the Seatonian poems.

> He rais'd the lame, the lepers he made whole,
>   He fix'd the palsied nerves of weak decay,
> He drove out Satan from the tortur'd soul,
>   And to the blind gave or restor'd the day—
> Nay more,—far more unequall'd pangs sustain'd
> Till his lost fallen flock his taintless blood regain'd.

> My feeble feet refus'd my body's weight,
>   Nor wou'd my eyes admit the glorious light,
> My nerves convuls'd shook fearful of their fate,
>   My mind lay open to the powers of night.
> He pitying did a second birth bestow,
> A birth of joy—not like the first of tears and woe.

Ye strengthen'd feet, forth to his altar move;
    Quicken, ye new-strung nerves, th' enraptur'd lyre;
Ye heav'n-directed eyes, o'erflow with love;
    Glow, glow my soul, with pure seraphic fire;
Deeds, thoughts, and words no more his mandates break,
But to his endless glory work, conceive, and speak.

These are from the *Hymn to the Supreme Being* which
Smart wrote and published after his recovery in that year;
the theme is taken from the story of King Hezekiah who was
reprieved at the point of death and given a new lease of life
that he might devote it wholly to God. The *Hymn* is of the
utmost importance. It shows us a man who is in fact on the
brink of religious mania, yet whose intentions are completely
sane, poised and lucid. He has no hare-brained scheme in
mind; he is still devoted to his young wife and passionately
fond of his little daughters; he is simply going to consecrate
his hitherto-frustrated creative genius to the praise and service of God. He has received the immortal inspiration; all he
needs is the proper vehicle to express it. For that purpose he
throws off the urban sophistication that has been sitting
uneasily on his verse since boyhood; he goes humbly back
to the beginning as it were, that is, back a century and a half
to the period when English religious verse began its great
essor. Inevitably the beginnings are somewhat clumsy but the
power is there. The first of these stanzas might have come
straight out of Robert Southwell's *Peter's Playnt*, except that
the last line is an Alexandrine like Spenser's:

I sent back memory, in heedful guise,
    To search the record of preceding years;
Home, like the raven to the ark, she flies,
    Croaking bad tidings to my trembling ears.
O Sun, again that thy retreat was made,
And threw my follies back into the friendly shade!

But who are they, that bid affliction cease!—
    Redemption and forgiveness, heavenly sounds!
Behold the dove that brings the branch of peace,
    Behold the balm that heals the gaping wounds.
Vengeance divine's by pentitence supprest—
She struggles with the angel, conquers, and is blest.

Yet hold, presumption, nor too fondly climb,
   And thou too hold, O horrible despair!
In man humility's alone sublime,
   Who diffidently hopes he's *Christ's* own care—
O all-sufficient Lamb! in death's dread hour
Thy merits who shall slight, or who can doubt thy power?

But soul-rejoicing health again returns,
   The blood meanders gentle in each vein,
The lamp of life renew'd with vigour burns,
   And exil'd reason takes her seat again—
Brisk leaps the heart, the mind's at large once more,
To love, to praise, to bless, to wonder and adore.

The virtuous partner of my nuptial bands,
   Appear'd a widow to my frantic sight;
My little prattlers lifting up their hands,
   Beckon me back to them, to life, and light;
I come, ye spotless sweets! I come again,
Nor have your tears been shed, nor have ye knelt in vain.

As the *Hymn* draws to an end it gains in clarity; he tells the world exactly what he is going to do, and it is clear that he has sustained a true religious conversion. He is struck down by penitence, then lifted up by hope and zeal to make amends, then both penitence and zeal bow down before charity:

O! penitence to virtue near allied,
   Thou can'st new joys e'en to the blest impart;
The list'ning angels lay their harps aside
   To hear the music of thy contrite heart;
And heav'n itself wears a more radiant face,
When charity presents thee to the throne of grace . . .

Thus in high heaven charity is great,
   Faith, hope, devotion, hold a lower place;
On her the cherubs and the seraphs wait,
   Her, every virtue courts, and every grace;
See! on the right, close by th' Almighty's throne,
In him she shines confest, who came to make her known.

Deep-rooted in my heart then let her grow,
   That for the past the future may atone;
That I may act what thou hast given to know,
   That I may live for THEE and THEE alone,
And justify those sweetest words from Heav'n,
'THAT HE SHALL LOVE THEE MOST TO WHOM
   THOU'ST MOST FORGIVEN.'

The greater part of the *Hymn* has been quoted here because it is Smart's perfectly serious *apologia* for his change of life. We should not take it any the less seriously because it was published as a naive token of gratitude to Dr James and his fever-powders which had now cured Smart for the third time. Smart was a naive person; Dr James was a most respected physician; many people regarded his fever-powders with an almost religious trust. Nor should we think any the less of Newbery, the publisher, because he combined an act of piety with a good piece of advertisement.

Newbery had not taken any deep offence at Smart's contract with the *Universal Visitor*. He not only published this poem and republished the *Seatonian*, but he and Carnan kept advertising the appearance of the *Tales and Fables in Verse*. Meanwhile Johnson agreed to write for the *Visitor* during Smart's illness, letting the profit go to his family. It was an act of considerable generosity on Johnson's part, even though he passed it off with a typically caustic comment: "I wrote for some months in the *Universal Visitor* for poor Smart when he was mad, not then knowing the terms on which he was engaged to write, and thinking I was doing him good. I hoped his wits would soon return to him. Mine returned to me, and I wrote in the *Universal Visitor* no longer."

Now comes the sad part of the story.

When Smart had apparently recovered his health in the late Spring of 1756, there was much rejoicing among his family and plans for some work that would be lucrative but not too heavy, such as adding a few more fables to the collection that was overdue. Smart refused; he also refused to write for the *Visitor*; he refused to write anything which was not directly and explicitly in praise of God. Then he went further. He said that it was God's command that we should pray continually. He began to pray continually, not in private meditation, but out loud—vociferously—in public. The terrifying part was that he appeared quite sane. During his illness there had been periods of delirium when he was out of his wits. But now he knew quite clearly what he was doing. There are several entries in his later writing, *Jubilate Agno*, which attest this; for example: "The Lord direct me in the better way going on in the Fifth year of my jeopardy June ye 17th. N.S. 1760." By "jeopardy" Smart meant the sufferings and confinement which came upon him as a result of his "confessing God openly." Thus this extraordinary entry of 1760 tells us also that it was in June of 1756 that his activities reached a stage where forcible restraint had to be put upon him.

Later on, I will try to explain the working of Smart's mind, drawing on *Jubilate Agno* for evidence and also on the comments of Dr Johnson and Mrs Thrale. At present we are concerned only with the external facts so far as they are known. "My poor friend Smart," said Johnson to Boswell on their first meeting in May 1763, "showed the disturbance of his mind by falling upon his knees and saying his prayers in the street or in any other unusual place." "He insisted," he had said earlier, "on people praying with him." Mrs Thrale is more detailed and interesting, though she may have got most of her information from Johnson.

> While Kit Smart thought it his duty to pray in Secret, no living creature knew how mad he was; but as soon as the Idea struck him that every time he thought of praying, Resistance against that divine Impulse (as he thought it) was a Crime: he knelt down in the Streets & Assembly Rooms, and wherever he was when the thought crossed his mind—and this indecorous conduct obliged his Friends to place him in a Confinement whence many mad as he remain excluded, only because their *Delusion* is not known.

Elsewhere she adds that Smart's madness

> shewed itself only in a preternatural excitement to prayer, which he held it as a duty not to controul or repress—taking *au pied de la lettre* our blessed Saviour's injunction to *pray without ceasing.*—So that beginning by regular addresses to the Almighty, he went on to call his friends from their dinners, or beds, or places of recreation, whenever that impulse to prayer pressed upon his mind.

So it began at regular times, but in any place; in the mall, in the coffee-house, at the play, Smart's voice—an extraordinarily deep and resonant voice for so small a person— might boom forth in ecstatic and persistent litany. Then it went on to any time; at any moment, in the middle of dinner, in the middle of the night even, there could be a clamour at the door and there he would stand, the little man, steadfast and smiling: "Hallelujah! Let us bless the Lord without ceasing!"

Hearty laughter at Kit's quaint humour changed to nervous laughter at his intensity, nervous laughter changed to frightened expostulation, expostulation to panic, panic to despair. Those who were not his friends, people like Griffiths' cut-throats of the *Monthly Review*, began to say "The man should be in Bedlam! *Take him to Bedlam!*"

What made Smart's "conversion" in a way more distressing was that it was so uncharacteristically dreary and unoriginal. For more than a century now a string of weak-headed prophets had been inflicting their private revelations upon the public; and public opinion whether Laudian or Erastian, Anglican or Dissenting, of whatever degree of piety or indifference, had definitely decided "No!" The Methodists were the latest and the most formidable. It is true that Wesley and Whitfield were beginning to be accepted in certain circles—Wesley as a saintly religious leader, Whitfield as a fashionable preacher. But to the greater part of the nation—including all Smart's London circle—Methodists were just religious disturbers, or a form of Bedlamites, whose common trade-mark was obstreperous public prayer and unhealthy effervescence. In sentencing a Methodist preacher (a false one as it turned out), Northington, the Lord Chancellor of 1757, said: "Bigotry and enthusiasm have spread their baneful influence far and wide, and the unhappy objects of the contagion almost daily increase. Of this, not only Bedlam, but most of the private madhouses, are melancholy and striking proofs." Smart was in real danger.

It was an added peril that his wife was a Roman Catholic. A Catholic was still the stock type of religious extravagance. In Hogarth's terrible painting of Bedlam, the typical religious maniac is a Papist praying to his images. "Methodists, Papists, and other disturbers of the Kingdom of God," said Gibson, late Bishop of London; and of the two, "Papist" was much the more dangerous label because none of the ferocious penal laws against them had yet been repealed. Many of the enlightened middle class—men like Stevens

(Lord Mayor of London), Samuel Johnson, Murray (Lord Mansfield) and Newbery (as has been pointed out)—had shaken off the old bigotry. But the first repeal did not come till 1779. The attitude of the Government was the same that Trajan expressed in his letter to Pliny about the Christians in Bithinia: *Non conquirendi sunt*, "Do not hunt them out, but if they thrust themselves on your notice, then the law must take its course." The death-penalty would never again be invoked, but a common informer could still claim £100 reward for discovering a priest. In 1764 a man called Payne decided to practise this trade in the Moorfields chapel (which passed as a private hotel) where the Islington Catholics worshipped. The *Museum* for 21 October 1765 records: "two Romish priests were taken out of a private house in Moorfields to be dealt with according to the law"; and in 1767 Father John-Baptist Maloney was sentenced to penal servitude for life for saying Mass. Smart's "enthusiasm" could easily have put his wife in grave danger. Her uncle, Father Hounshill, who had been imprisoned during the '45, may well have been in the London district at this time, for Newbery bequeathed him money in his will of 1763.

So it came about that on 17 June 1756—as far as we can ascertain—Newbery and Carnan turned the key on Christopher Smart with the consent of all his relatives. It was the only way to save him from being whisked off to Bedlam by some ill-disposed magistrate, and from awkward inquiries being made into the religion of young Mrs Smart and her mother.

It was customary, in situations like these, to keep the sufferer for as long as possible in his own home to see if reason would prevail. No doubt the parson from St Mary's, Canonbury, was called in, and possibly other clergymen of Smart's acquaintance. If so, they made not the least apparent impression on him. If his wife made any impression, it seems from subsequent references to have been one of hostility. She, poor soul, could only fall back on the ancient wisdom of her Church; that all private revelations must be tested by obedience to lawful authority. "For," as the author of *The Imitation of Christ* said, centuries earlier, echoing this ancient wisdom, "not every desire is from the Holy Spirit, though to men it seem right and good. It is difficult to judge truly whether it be a good or evil spirit that impels you to desire this or that, or whether you are not moved to it by your own spirit. Many have been deceived in the end, who at first seemed to be led by a good spirit." But, confronted with the mysteries of private judgment in spiritual matters, she could do nothing except pray silently in opposition to her husband's vociferous prayer.

Eventually, after much suffering, Smart learned to do the same; Mrs Thrale wrote of him as she knew him eight or ten years later: "he calmed every violent start of passion by prayer," that is, by quiet prayer he calmed the excitements to loud prayer. But at first he yielded completely to these excitements, "these temporary alienations of mind" as Hunter called them; and these, when checked or opposed, "were at last attended by paroxysms so violent and continued as to render confinement necessary." So there are evidently three elements to be distinguished in the new Smart: first, the impulse to pray in general, which is surely a good thing; secondly, the "alienations of mind" when he went off to pray in public, yet still apparently retaining full possession of his faculties, and, thirdly, the violent paroxysms when he was right out of his wits.

And now, before going on to write of Smart's physical confinement, I feel compelled by two crushing certainties to find out what lies between the two certainties. There is the certainty that his conversion was genuine, from God; and there is the certainty that the excitements to prayer that led to these paroxysms were delusions, not from God. So I feel compelled to try and discover what went wrong between the "good spirit" of his conversion and the "bad spirit" of delusion. I will write of course not as an amateur physician, still less as an amateur psychiatrist—for I have observed when literary men start discussing "schizophrenia" and "cyclothymes" and so on, the result is an embarrassing confusion and abuse of words—but as a spiritual adviser after the fact. For if, as I think can be be clearly shown, Smart was in full possession of his faculties when he embraced his delusion, then the crux of his malady was spiritual, rather than mental or bodily. Between the conception and the act, then, what shadow fell?

Several shadows, long ones: they reach out and fall discernibly across the pages of *Jubilate Agno*. But this was written several years after the point we have reached. So the rest of this chapter will indicate only the sort of shadows that may be expected. It will involve a consideration of Smart's conversion and of the spiritual life in general. It will be a didactic sort of consideration; but for those who can bear it, even if they do not agree with it, it will at least guarantee some clarity.

The impulses that move and carry a man on to a higher kind of life are many and varied. But those that Smart records in his *Hymn* are very typical and, in any case, the most convenient to describe. First, there is the impulse of dissatisfaction with one's self. Many people feel this now and again, and let it pass away like a puff of smoke. But if you are open to receive it deeply, and then hold it and deepen it still further by thoughtful consideration, you are embarked upon what Christian writers from very ancient times have called the penitential or "The Purgative Way." You discover a "sense of God," that is, a profound awareness that you depend utterly upon God your Creator, who is the unfathomable source of your existence, and so of your every thought and action; you discover also a "sense of sin," a basic horror at the prospect of dislocation from the source of your being, who is also, objectively, the substantial source of all goodness and holiness. It is important that this way should be pursued with the mind firmly in control of the emotions; otherwise you would be swamped by horrible fantasies of despair. Smart was well aware of this danger and avoided it. But an imaginative and volatile man, even avoiding despair, could not remain indefinitely in this way, nor would he be intended to.

The shaft of grace from God is like a rocket which carries a second (and also a third) delayed charge in it. After the explosion of penitence which frees you from the pull of mundane values, there is a second impulse or infusion of light and warmth in which you see your ideal self and are delightfully attracted and spurred on to become that ideal self. You see yourself "in Christ"; for Christ's human nature, with the infinite godhead shining through it, is the model and ideal of every human being; each human personality is a facet of Christ's divine personality. This is what is called "The Illuminative Way," in which you follow Christ, transplanting the scenes of the gospel into your imagination and mind and heart. A very common sequel of this impulse to follow Christ is the desire to preach Christ to others, to communicate your inspiration, to be a friend of Christ as the Apostles were. But this branch of the Illuminative Way is the most open to danger and delusion; for it is very hard to distinguish between the good self-love, which is love of one's ideal self, that is of Christ; and the self-love which is love of self, *tout court*, and may lead through vanity and selfishness to the most appalling arrogance and megalomania. Therefore the Illuminative Way must always be paralleled by the Purgative Way, so that one may get to know one's hidden weaknesses more and more clearly, and be grounded more and more deeply in humility. Smart was well aware of this danger also, as he shows in the lines already quoted:

> Yet hold, presumption, nor too fondly climb,
> And thou too hold, O horrible despair!
> In man humility's alone sublime,
> Who diffidently hopes he's *Christ's* own care—

He was aware of it in theory, that is, but unfortunately he forgot it in practice. No man should dare to consider himself an emissary of God until he has been through a sort of noviceship and resolved certain conflicts within himself or at least reached a *modus vivendi* in which he is as acutely conscious of his own weakness as he is of the power of God to help him.

People sometimes point to the example of Christ's Apostles who started preaching immediately after receiving the Holy Ghost, as if that was a justification for every self-appointed preacher. But Pentecost was the unique public revelation for all time, it was the entire cup filled up, pressed down and running over. Quite apart from that, the Apostles had already

85

been through two or three years' hard training from Our Lord himself; they were already hardened campaigners and, what is more, they had received during the days from Thursday to Easter Sunday an unforgettable lesson of their own weakness and the power of God. Even Paul of Tarsus, after his miraculous conversion, felt the need to retire into Arabia for a good part of three years, and all the great preachers, St Basil, St Bernard, St Francis Xavier, have had the same sort of noviceship. Without something of the sort, you get the half-baked preacher who pitchforks his own unrealized temptations on to other people or makes divine edicts out of his own prejudices and resentments. It is better for such a man if he is made a failure and a fool of, as Smart was, instead of becoming a success and a scandal.

Smart's paroxysms showed him up as a deluded fool. But it was not God who had deluded him. Nor did God desert him.

There is a third stage in the shaft of grace which God communicates to the soul. The first is abasement of the old self, the second is the realization of a new and better self. The third is forgetfulness of self altogether; both one's vices and one's virtues disappear from view, there is room only for the glory of God. It is an impulse which in its natural form comes sometimes, for example, to mountaineers. In its supernatural form it is pure charity: the love of God with no mixture of self-interest, but just because he is what he is. This is what is called "The Unitive Way"; but to achieve it as a *way* is very hard. Complete forgetfulness of self as an impulse or for a short time is one thing; as a permanent outlook on life it is quite another. You only have to try it to see.

Only very great saints have achieved it, and generally as a result or accompaniment of very great suffering. Nevertheless, even only as an impulse or for a short time, it is enormously beneficial to be "taken out of one's self," to be lifted above one's depression or complacency, to share in a manner God's infinitely benevolent view of all his creatures.

Smart was one of those spiritually gifted persons who are open to receive this blessed impulse frequently. At first, as may be remembered, he called it "good-nature." Then he came to call it the Angel of Gratitude or the Seraph of

Charity. The more he suffered as a result of his supposed lunacy, the more frequent were these visitations to console and strengthen him.

But, of course, he was far from achieving the Unitive Way as a way of life, because of unresolved conflicts festering within him. It is these which cast their shadows over the pure praises and blessings of the *Jubilate Agno*. There is, for example, an Othello-like jealousy, a morbid preoccupation with horns and cuckoldry, coupled with extravagant misogyny. Then there is a crazy search for spiritual credentials for himself, involving him in Gnostic and "British Israelitic" genealogies. There is also a bitterness against Rome, seemingly irrational and quite foreign to his tolerant and happy nature. This last may have been the source of the other two, of the anger against his wife and of the search for spiritual credentials.

Whatever may have been the cause of his obsessions, it deprived him of the peace of soul which should have resulted from his conversion. If the "good spirit" of his conversion had been allowed to work, he would have sought first the kingdom of God within himself; he would have possessed his soul in patience and fulfilled the immediate duties of his state. As to God's will for him in the future, he would have sought light in quiet prayer and in the counsel of wise and holy advisers.

But something—some fear of what he would find, perhaps —made him shrink from seeking within himself. Instead, he allowed himself to be driven out in a loud and turbulent manner to preach to others and to assume the guises of an arrogant pseudo-prophet. That was what "went wrong" in the period of sanity after his conversion and before his confinement.

It remains to be seen from the continuing pages of *Jubilate Agno*, and from his actions afterwards, how far he recognized the falsity of his position and how far the inspiration of charity was able to save him and restore him to peace with God and himself.

But in the meantime the external story of his "jeopardy" and confinement must first be told.

SEVEN

❖

At St Luke's Asylum

THE Committee Book of St Luke's records that the "petitions and certificates" for the admission of Christopher Smart were read on 18 March 1757; and that after some delays he was brought up for examination and admitted on 6 May.

St Luke's Hospital for the insane, near Old Street in Shoreditch, was a new asylum founded in 1750 by a committee of wealthy London philanthropists and opened in 1751. Lunacy was becoming a national problem, either because lunatics were in fact alarmingly on the increase, or else because their plight was becoming much more noticed. The foundation of St Luke's was in response to a feeling that they were not cared for at all adequately by existing institutions.

The only other public madhouse was the ancient hospital of Bethlehem or Bedlam in Moorfields, where conditions, faithfully depicted by Hogarth in the eighth and last scene of *The Rake's Progress*, are almost too notorious to need description. From reforms which were introduced later in the century it seems that in Smart's time chains were left in position till limbs mortified, unchanged straw was allowed to gather damp and filth indefinitely, dysentery and scurvy were taken for granted. Perhaps the most notorious abuse was the custom of "visiting days" when sightseers could file past and poke up the lunatics at will so as to have a good laugh at their frenzies. Bad characters of every kind could get in on these days to ply their trades or pursue their crooked inclinations.

Even high-minded men like Dr Johnson and William Cowper could not resist the morbid attraction of observing subjects who had gone farther along the fatal road than themselves. It is a relief to know that almost certainly Smart never saw the inside of this place as an inmate—only perhaps as a visitor on the occasion described in *The Midwife* of 1751.

Apart from Bedlam, which was free, the only other asylums were the so-called "private madhouses" where patients could be lodged by their relatives for a fee which might vary between twenty and a hundred guineas a year. There were a great number of these places, most of them quite small, housing not more than half a dozen lunatics each, run by a married couple without any kind of medical supervision—though the owner who collected the profit would usually be some larger moneyed figure in the background. Hoxton was the area near London where these houses were most frequent. Dr Arthur Morris, author of *The Hoxton Madhouses*, quotes Andrew Marvell who said of an opponent in 1672, "he is fit for nothing but *Bedlam* or *Hogsdon*." It is difficult to generalize about what went on inside the private madhouses in Smart's time. There was no thorough public inquiry until the Select Committee of 1815—which is the main subject of *The Hoxton Madhouses*. What was there revealed varied from a chamber of horrors where violent and non-violent were herded together in sickening cruelty and degradation to a quiet little hostel of relative comfort and security. There was probably the same sort of variety half a century earlier. Little positive evidence is available. There was an occasional lurid revelation as, for example, in 1739 when Alexander Cruden, author of the famous *Concordance*, escaped at midnight, stark naked and fully manacled, out of a window and over the wall of Wright's madhouse in Bethnal Green. There was also a partial inquiry by the House of Commons into private madhouses in January 1763, the very month in which Smart was released, but that must wait till the year of his life when it most applies. What was common to nearly all these private asylums was that there was no check on who was "admitted," or bundled in; there was no regular medical attendance while they were inside; no questions asked when they died.

The foundation of St Luke's was a noble effort to avoid the evils of the private houses as well as to offer some alternative to the public horrors of Bedlam. Cleanliness and constant attention were to be insisted on; violence was not to be used as a general rule, but only with discretion; above all, there was to be no vulgar sightseeing; instead there was a general invitation to all members of the faculty to come and study cases and compare methods. The superintendent chosen to institute and personify all these reforms was a distinguished member of the College of Physicians, Dr William Battie.

No facetious playing upon words should be allowed to obscure the character and qualities of Dr Battie. He was the essence of sanity. His premises concerning the nature of madness were empirically based and accorded with the new philosophy of ideas, but his conclusions from them flowed with Aristotelian calm and certainty. A lunatic by his definition is one who insistently sees things that are not really there. A man, for example, receives a blow upon the nose: he sees stars; if he judges those stars to be real and not imaginary, he is a lunatic. Another man sees an image of himself as King Charles I without a head; if he judges that to represent the reality about himself, he is likewise a lunatic. In both cases the remoter cause of the hallucination is an undue pressure upon the nervous matter of the brain which it will be the physician's task to locate, if possible, and to relieve.

Dr Battie was a Cambridge man, a holder of the Craven scholarship as Smart had been, though of an earlier vintage— he was born in 1704. When he was chosen for St Luke's, he was at the height of his professional success, earning as much as £1,000 a year in fees. One of his sidelines was a private madhouse in Wood's Close near Islington, but he owned it under a different name so as to avoid the danger of prosecution. In the inquiry of 1815 it was revealed that the Master of St Luke's of that time used to transfer patients between his paying private house and the non-paying public hospital. If Battie did the same in his day, then it is more than likely that Smart was in his Islington private house before he was admitted to St Luke's. It is unlikely that he was shut up in his own house for all that first year. Battie might well be the "Doctor of my Acquaintance who keeps a private House" referred to in the *Midwife* article.

But in any case Smart was certainly under his sole care for a year, from May 1757 till May 1758 when he was discharged. So it is important to know something about Battie's character and about his theories; it will tell us a little about how Smart would have been treated during that year, and also perhaps a little more about the nature of his ailment.

Battie's character is quite well described by his friends who supplied the information for his biography in Nichols' *Literary Anecdotes*. He had evidently a bland, omniscient professional manner which concealed a lively mind well aware of its own limitations and an eccentric, griggish sense of humour. His friends were easily able to get behind the façade and poke fun at him. "No truth," wrote one informant, "in the story of his going to be put into the kettle or boiling copper by some of the maniacs who had lain hands upon him with that intent." He is known to have played the fool in order to distract the fixed melancholia of one of his patients. His enemies misjudged his assumed pomposity as hypocrisy and deceit. In a paper war against the College of Physicians he was especially singled out and was roughly handled by a professional scribbler in a squib called *The Battiad*:

> In mischief mighty, though but mean of size,
> And, like the Tempter, ever in disguise.
> See him with aspect grave and gentle tread
> By slow degrees approach the sickly bed:
> Then at his club behold him altered soon,
> The solemn Doctor turns a low buffoon.

There may have been, one suspects, something of the charlatan or at least of the cynic about Dr Battie, but in spite of that, or maybe even because of it, he was essentially a broadminded, good-tempered and kindly man—very different from the bristling tyrants of the Monro family who lorded it over Bedlam.

Battie's theories and methods were set forth in his *Treatise on Madness*, published—very appositely—in 1758. He opens with a Panglossian sentence in which he takes nearly a page to say that, since we cannot know what causes true ideas of existing things to arise in the brain of a normal person, so we cannot know what causes chimaeras to arise in the brain of a madman. We can, however, he continues, discover remoter external aggravations—like the blow on the nose already mentioned—which produce images of non-existing things. So he distinguishes two kinds of madness: one caused solely by intrinsic weakness of the brain, the other attributable to remoter external aggravations. The first is Original Madness and it is incurable. "Original Madness whether it be hereditary or intermittent is not removable by any method which the science of Physick in its present imperfect state is able to suggest." The second is Consequential Madness, and it may have a variety of external causes, all of which will be some form or other of pressure on the brain. To diagnose the kind of pressure and to prescribe the proper way of relieving it will be the first steps towards curing or at least alleviating the madness, provided the madness is "consequential" from this external pressure, and not due to "original" or intrinsic weakness.

Among seven or eight different kinds of pressure, Battie has two particularly connected with religious mania. One is the congestion or constriction which goes with a melancholic fixation of mind.

> To such constant muscular constriction and to the gradual or chronical congestion in the brain or mesenteric viscera thereby occasioned, the despairing bigot incapable in his own apprehension of being pardoned, or predestined by infinite justice to eternal misery before he had a being, the moping lover, the motionless widow or mother bereft of her children, may at first view be ascribed.

This melancholia, however, was not the form which Smart's religious feelings took. The other form, much more applicable to Smart, is spasm or muscular convulsion; hence we see

> that madness frequently succeeds or accompanies Fever, Epilepsy, Childbirth and the like muscular disorders; and that the tumultuous and visibly spasmodic passions of joy and anger are all at least for a time maniacal. But these passions constringe the muscles of the head

and neck, and therefore like a ligature force the blood that was descending in the jugular veins back upon the minutest vessels of the brain.

It seems very likely that this is how Battie judged the "paroxysms" of which Hunter speaks; especially as Smart was subject to recurring fever.

It is possible that alcohol aggravated the disorder; but I do not think there is any justification for Mr Stead's comment quoted in the first chapter, that Smart "mingled his prayers with strong drink; he prayed, and got drunk; he prayed again, and then he got drunk again." I have already given some reasons, and will give some more later on, for dismissing this conjecture—although, like most conjectures, it remains a possibility.

Discussing spasm and convulsion further, Battie says that it is more dangerous than the congestion of melancholia but also more curable.

When spasm is productive of obstructions upon the brain and nerves, and in this case becomes another and remoter cause of Consequential Madness, if such spasm is suddenly excited either by the tumultuous passions of joy and anger, or by intoxicating drugs and vinous spirits, it is indeed very violent and oftentimes fatal by its immediate effects. But in case the patient is capable of bearing the first shock and has not been weakened by frequent attacks of the same nature; such sudden and irregular action of the muscles together with all its phrenetic or maniacal consequences is much sooner either spontaneously abated or relieved by art, than the gradual and continued muscular constriction which is occasioned by the more gentle passions of love, grief and despair, or by long and uninterrupted attention to any one object, however pleasing and agreeable.

The remedies proposed by Dr Battie for convulsive madness are quite different from those for congestive madness or melancholia. For melancholia he agrees that violent shocks are necessary to distract the patient's desperate attention to one thing: caustics, emetics, rough cathartics and bodily pain. But for convulsion he does not agree with the usual opinion. The usual opinion was that violent spasms of joy or anger must be broken by the counter-violence of an opposing emotion; wild anger must be beaten into terror, joy into sorrow, and so on. That is the way the poor King, George III, was treated by the scoundrels who had charge of him.

Battie, however, believed that drugs and sedatives were the only things that were of any use in cases like that. If he had been quite frank, he would probably have said that nothing was really of very much use, so why add unnecessary cruelty? In one of his pleasantly human asides he remarks:

> Madness, like several other animal distempers, oftentimes ceases spontaneously, that is, without our being able to assign a sufficient reason; and many a Lunatick, who by the reception of vomits and other convulsive stimuli would have been strained into downright Idiotism, has when given over as incurable recovered his understanding.

In some ways, therefore, Smart was fortunate to have been admitted into St Luke's instead of being sent to Bedlam or to one of the more sordid private houses, and he probably owed that to Newbery. He was recommended by a Mr Francis Gosling, a prosperous bookseller who had become a banker: probably a friend of Newbery's and probably also one of the Governors of St Luke's, since these were mostly bankers.

He seems to have some reminiscences of kindly physical treatment in a passage of *Jubilate Agno* written three years later:

> For the Bark was a communication from God and is sovereign.
> For the method of curing an ague by terror is exaction . . .
> For an Ague is the terror of the body, when the blessing of God is with-held for a season.
> For benevolence is the best remedy in the first place and the bark in the second.[1]

He had learned to dread the "ague" or recurring fever which made him more liable to spasms and convulsions. Battie, it will be remembered, held that frenzy often followed or accompanied fever. It is likely that Smart is remembering St Luke's in this passage, for a little further on he prays God "to be gracious to Livemore [*sic*] my fellow prisoner"; Ezra Livermore or Levermore was in St Luke's in 1758 and afterwards in Bedlam.

"Prisoner" is a harsh word for Smart to use. But it is true in the sense that Battie's rules of confinement were very

---

[1] The "bark" is quinine. "Exaction" is Smart's word for an utter lack of mercy—exacting a pound of flesh.

strict. Not only the visits of sightseers but also of family and dear friends were forbidden, lest disturbing memories be aroused.

> The visits therefore of affecting friends as well as enemies, and the impertinent curiosity of those who think it pastime to converse with Madmen and to play upon their passions, ought strictly to be forbidden.
>
> On the same account the place of confinement should be at some distance from home, and, let him be where he will, none of his own servants should be suffered to wait on him.

So it is very unlikely that Smart saw his wife and children during that period.

But the most important fact we know about Smart's stay in St Luke's is that after a year, on 12 May 1758, he was discharged as "incurable." The Committee Book records:

> Dr Battie having acquainted this Committee that Christopher Smart continues disordered in his senses notwithstanding he has been admitted into this Hospital above 12 Calendar Months and from the present Circumstances of his Case there being not sufficient reason to expect his speedy Recovery and he being brought up and examined: Ordered that he be discharged and that Notice be sent to his securities to take him away.[1]

The Committee Book further records that at the request of his friends he was placed "upon the Incurable List" to be re-admitted when there was a vacancy, on payment of five shillings a week; that is, his name was kept on the books on a waiting list, but if re-admitted as an "incurable" he would have to pay, whereas the "curables" were kept free of charge. This reads very much as if he went back to Dr Battie's private house, at least for some months, for he does not seem to have been back with his family or friends before the beginning of 1759.

It seems strange at first that Battie should have discharged him uncured, whereas his nephew in his memoir says: "After

[1] I am much indebted to the kindness of Dr Richard Hunter for these extracts from the St Luke's Committee Book. Other records, including the mention of Francis Gosling noted by Mr Stead in 1938, were unfortunately destroyed in the Second World War.

an interval of little more than two years, Mr Smart appeared to be pretty well restored, and was accordingly set at liberty; but his mind had received a shock from which it never entirely recovered."[1]

But there is really no discrepancy between Battie's "incurable" and Hunter's "appeared to be pretty well restored." Smart had learned, or was learning, from experience to check the excitements to public prayer which could end in paroxysms of joy or anger. But he had in no way altered his conviction that he had been chosen by God for some special purpose ("For by the grace of God," he wrote later in *Jubilate Agno*, "I am the Reviver of ADORATION amongst ENGLISH-MEN").

In Battie's philosophy there was no room, outside monasteries and madhouses, for special messages from heaven. Smart was obstinately imagining a state of things which did not exist; he was the equivalent of the man who sees stars floating in broad daylight and insists that they are real; he was a lunatick—only in his case there was no discernible exterior cause. His delusions had not been changed by any of the treatments for "consequential madness"; he was therefore, as far as could be ascertained, suffering from "original madness"—that is, from intrinsic and incurable brain-weakness, probably hereditary. It may have been this verdict which Smart was contemptuously dismissing when he wrote:

> For Silly fellow! Silly fellow! is against me and belongeth neither to me nor to my family.

A line or two further on he may be referring to the physicians and other authorities who were brought in to examine him before he was dismissed as incurable:

[1] Some writers on Smart think that Hunter was referring to the second period of confinement which lasted about three and a half years, from August 1759 to 30 January 1763. But Hunter, though studiously vague, was not grossly inaccurate; "a little more than two" cannot be made to mean three and a half, whereas if, as is very probable, Smart was transferred from Battie's private house to St Luke's and back again, his total period under Battie's care would have been a little more than two years—from the latter part of 1756 to the end of 1758.

For they pass by me in their tour, and the good Samaritan is not yet come.[1]

It must be admitted that though Battie may have benefited what he called Smart's "animal life," he had no effect upon his mind except to drive him more and more in upon himself. Battie lived far outside the Papist world (and the Wesleyan world for that matter) which believed in the "discernment of spirits," and long before the age of psycho-therapy. Spiritual guidance of the mentally afflicted had stopped with the reformation—though there had been a short intermittent period when Bedlam had its chaplains, notably the high-church Dean Atterbury. St Luke's from the beginning, in spite of its name, had no chaplain and no chapel. Howard, the great prison reformer, commented on this lack in 1788; it would have been an advantage at least, he thought, for those patients who were beginning to recover their wits.[2]

Battie's philosophy, as well as his spiritual outlook, was utterly foreign to Smart. Both as a believer and as a poet, Smart rejected the Lockean theory that the mind is a *tabula rasa*, a blank sheet, until ideas are stamped upon it by sense-objects. He believed, and in a way experienced, that the soul with its powers of knowing and loving was a living image of its Creator's knowledge and love. The mind at birth was already filled with hidden knowledge of God which only needed to be clarified by the senses and by speech. As a Christian—his particular type of Christian, I mean—how could he begin to look for God in creatures unless he had already an inward sense of what he was looking for? As a creative artist, it was not his part just to *receive* impressions but to *make* them, to create the pattern that was born within him. As a Christian artist it was his duty to stamp the likeness of God on all his

[1] At first sight this looks like a description of the sightseers in Bedlam; but since it is practically certain that Smart was never an inmate there, it seems more likely to be a reminiscence of St Luke's evoked by the thought of hereditary madness.

[2] Not that Battie did not claim to be a devout Christian. Quite the contrary. His last words to his death-bed attendant are reported as being "Young man . . . may you learn, and may you profit by the example, that a conscientious endeavour to perform his duty through life will ever close a Christian's eyes with comfort and tranquillity." An enviable example indeed.

field of knowledge in the medium that was most native to him, the medium of words.

> For Jacob's Ladder are the steps of the Earth graduated hence to Paradice and thence to the throne of God . . .
> For SPICA VIRGINIS is the star that appeared to the wise men in the East and directed their way before it was yet insphered.
> For an IDEA is the mental vision of an object.
> For Locke supposes that an human creature, at a given time may be an atheist i.e. without God, by the folly of his doctrine concerning innate ideas . . .
> For all the inventions of man, which are good, are the communications of Almighty God . . .
> For my talent is to give an impression upon words by punching, that when the reader casts his eye upon 'em, he takes up the image from the mould wch I have made.

These lines, all written close to each other in January 1760, are terribly and inevitably disjointed because the "Let" verses that went with them are missing; for example, there would obviously have been something about the Feast of the Epiphany to introduce the second verse about the star. Still, there is one current of thought running through them; they all revolve round Smart's poetic "Platonism"—to use that word for lack of a better. There is the Paradise of Ideas where the "Daughters of God" dwell—sons or daughters it makes no difference, they were both "Angels" to Smart. There is his clinging to the Platonic *anamnesis*, that stirring of the intellectual memory towards a certain vision of the outside world *before* it becomes broken and congealed into hard-and-fast terms.

Locke, of course, did not support atheism because he rejected innate ideas; and Smart, of course, did not hold that we were born with ideas (that is, distinct thoughts) already formed in us. But he did hold that since he (his soul) came into being stamped with the likeness of God, he was not a *tabula rasa*; and it was in his power to stamp that likeness upon the creatures in his field of knowledge in the very act of knowing them. (It is a tenet very much the same as Gerard Manley Hopkins's "inscape".)[1] Moreover it was his

[1] Some precise indications of this are given in J. B. Broadbent's introduction to his new edition of *A Song to David* (Bodley Head, 1960).

duty to represent these creatures in true and shining words before both words and creatures became debased by worldly commerce and "exaction."

So in the first three years of his confinement, a theory of poetry long felt obscurely within him began to take shape distinctly, the theory of "Impression."[1]

The constant turning-in upon himself during the two dreary years under Battie's charge did Smart both good and harm. He whittled down the knot of spiritual error noted in the last chapter, but what remained became harder and deeper and less possible to correct. As Mrs Thrale said, "he hugged his delusion in secret," instead of blatantly forcing it upon others. But what *was* this "delusion"?

It was something much saner and nearer to the core of his conversion. His original and good inspiration had been to devote his whole poetic power to the praise of God. His purpose now was to reform—or to revivify—the Catholic liturgy of the Church of England. With this purpose in mind he embarked upon the work which has been so often mentioned and quoted in this book: *Jubilate Agno*. Its distinction into "Let" and "For" verses was suggested by Dr Lowth's book on Hebrew poetry which he knew well: "One of the choirs sung a single verse to the other, while the other constantly added a verse in some respect correspondent to the former."

Mr Bond, the most recent editor of *Jubilate Agno*, writes:

He had been giving serious thought to a reformation of the Anglican liturgy. . . . it is more than probable that *Jubilate* was initially conceived as the opening move in this campaign of reform. That would explain why Smart found the principles outlined by Lowth peculiarly appropriate for his purposes. It is why the title and peroration of *Jubilate Agno* are so closely parallel to portions of the Order for Morning Prayer and the Psalter. The poem was intended as a responsive reading; and that is why the *Let* and *For* sections are physically distinct while corresponding verse for verse. Very few of the *Let* verses . . . contain references personal to Smart; these are nearly all confined to the *For*

[1] Mr Grigson makes an interesting suggestion that Smart's poetic theory of "Impression" may have owed something to a reading of Berkeley, e.g. such passages as "ideas imprinted on the senses are real things or do really exist."

99

verses. If, then, he visualized an actual performance of *Jubilate Agno*, it was apparently with himself as the second reader or responder.

If one misunderstood this last sentence, it would make Smart crazy enough for Bedlam. The choir of the Universal Church gives praise to God our Saviour—and Christopher Smart responds with some detail of his private life or experience. But he was not as mad as that. Nor can that be Mr Bond's meaning. In fact all the opening (Fragment A) "For" verses are missing; if they had survived, no doubt they would have been found to be as solemn and spiritual as the opening "Let" verses. But by the time the surviving "For" verses do start (Fragment B1), it is quite clear that Smart has abandoned the idea of *Jubilate Agno* as a public liturgical prayer and is continuing it as a kind of private spiritual diary. He had not, however, abandoned his purpose of reforming the liturgy.

Jubilate Agno cannot have been begun while Smart was at St Luke's, nor indeed while he was under Battie's care. No doubt he was brooding over the plan of it, but he would not have been allowed to put it down on paper. Any sort of intellectual pursuit likely to cause keen pleasure or anxiety was strictly forbidden by Battie's regime; only those occupations were encouraged which engaged the attention without absorbing it, like counting the lines in a page or copying down a list of names.[1]

So, before embarking upon *Jubilate Agno*, the chronicle of Smart's exterior life must be brought up to date, as far as that it possible, from the presumed date of his release from Dr Battie's care to the date of his second confinement.

---

[1] Smart may well have remembered Battie's advice during the last part of his second confinement; for that is more or less what he did in the last section of *Jubilate Agno* (Fragment D). Though cast in the form of invocations, with an occasional and invaluable personal interjection, it is really nothing but a list of names picked, apparently, from current periodicals.

EIGHT

❖

Jubilate Agno

IN January 1759 there was a notable stir of activity among
Smart's London friends which indicates that either he
was already set at liberty or was about to be so. David Garrick
on the 26th presented a "double bill" entirely for Smart's
benefit: *Merope*, adapted from Voltaire, and a new two-act
comedy called *The Guardian*, also from the French, adapted
by Garrick himself who played the principal part: "For the
Benefit of a Gentleman, well known in the Literary World,
who is at present under very unhappy Circumstances."

The first performance, at Drury Lane, was announced
in the *Public Advertiser* of 17 January. On the following day,
Thomas Gray, who happened to be in London, wrote in
surprise to his friend Mason that "poor Smart is not dead
as was said, & Merope is acted for his benefit this week with
a new Farce, the Guardian." Mason's reply is perhaps the
best indication that Smart had actually emerged into the land
of the living:

> This Resuscitation of Poor Smart pains me, I was in hopes he was
> safe in that state where the best of us will be better than we are &
> the worst I hope as little worse as infinite Justice can permit. But is he
> returned to his senses? if so, I fear that will be more terrible still,
> pray, if you can dispose of a Guinea so as it will in any sort benefit
> him (for 'tis too late for a ticket) give it to me.

Evidently Smart had been in confinement for the rest of
the year after he left St Luke's (in Battie's private house, as I
have conjectured) and evidently both Gray and Mason, before
they heard the false report of his death, had heard that he was

"incurable" and, probably that his new religious persuasions were a danger to himself and to his family. Now, however, he was at liberty; and Garrick's première looks like part of a campaign to find funds to provide for him.

If so, Newbery was in union with the scheme, for he and Carnan printed and published *The Guardian* in an octavo shilling volume immediately after its presentation, and there is evidence that he set aside other profits for his son-in-law. Other friends did their best, in the *Public Advertiser* and elsewhere, to make a great success of the benefit. And a great success it was; after the tickets had been sold out (as Mason's letter shows) there was still a fund open to receive guineas for the poet who had endeared himself to so many groups of friends.

Two things strike a reader about the printed tributes to Smart. First, in spite of the artificiality which clings to nearly all heroic couplets of that period, they do represent an extraordinary wave of affection *and admiration*. Arthur Murphy, that very honest and good-hearted fellow, spoke for all the intimate friends in the *Public Advertiser* of 3 February. Having praised all Smart's better-known poems, he goes on to pay a true and touching tribute to his generosity, his courage, his unswerving morality, his unquenchable joy:

> This Praise, my Friend, nor this thy Praise alone;
> A higher claim and nobler Wreaths you own,
> Thy wide Benevolence, thy Soul sincere,
> Thy generous Friendship, and thy social Tear,
> Thy Public Spirit that disdained a Slave;
> Thy honest Pride that still despised a Knave,
> Thy Manly Warmth each Rival to Commend;
> Thy Rapture to the merit of a Friend,
> Thy steady Morals that ne'er lost their Sway,
> Nor, like thy vernal Genius felt Decay,
> All this was thine; this it's Reversion brings
> When Wit and Poetry are idle Things.

Yet these fine lines are in the past tense. The second thing, striking like a dead weight, is the note of hopelessness and finality in the tributes. Richard Rolt lamented:

> Heart-piercing thought! no more these joys are mine;
> Thy elevated genius soared divine:
> And human nature dignified in thee
> Had almost shown us the Divinity:
> But Wisdom there was lost, and we deplore
> Thy loss, which ages never may restore.

A poetaster called Woty had no doubt that Smart would never write again:

> Unhappy Bard, whose elevated soul
> From earth took flight and reached the starry pole;
> Whose harp celestial lies in broken state;
> Affecting emblem of its master's fate!
> Ah me! no more, I fear, its tuneful strings,
> Touched by his hand, will praise the King of Kings.

While a Mr Lockman in the *Public Advertiser* voiced a fairly general opinion that religious fervour was highly displeasing to the Deity:

> Wrapt in a Vision, he presumed to sing
> The attributes of Heaven's Eternal King:
> But O! approaching towards the Throne of Light,
> Its flashing splendours overpowered his Sight.
> Hence blind on Earth, behold him sadly stray;
> 'Tis we must cheer the Horrors of his way.

How far Smart was conscious of his friends' generous help is something we cannot know. He seems to have gone on his way fairly satisfactorily for at least the first six months of this year, 1759, lodging in his former bachelor haunt by St James's Park. His place as Newbery's chief writer had been taken by Oliver Goldsmith, who had not yet produced any of his great works. Goldsmith was a warm admirer of Smart and had much the same attitude towards money and business; he found Newbery a fussy and exacting employer, but honest, friendly and appreciative—a very pleasant change after Griffiths. One of the hack jobs he was doing for Newbery was collecting the war news from the files of the *Reading Mercury* to form a "Martial Review" or history of the Seven Years War, then in its third year (its dates correspond exactly with those of Smart's "jeopardy," 1756–63). There is a generally accepted story that all the profits of the *Martial Review* were set aside for Smart or for his family.

Goldsmith, who was about to move into Canonbury House on the floor next to that given by Newbery to the Smart family, would have welcomed Smart as a fellow-lodger. But—and here we come to one of the most tragic and inexplicable things in his life—his wife, Anna-Maria, and the two little daughters were not living in England at the time he was set at liberty. They had left for Ireland in the previous year.

Mr Brittain has discovered a series of advertisements in the London *Gazeteer* from the beginning of January to the end of June 1759 showing that Mrs Smart had established herself in a shop in Dublin as a vendor for Newbery of Dr James's powders. Mrs Thrale has an anecdote about Mrs Smart dining with Mr George Falkiner, a Dublin bookseller, while she was selling the powders. It is generally accepted by early writers on Smart that she stayed with her husband's sister and brother-in-law, Richard Falkiner, a Dublin barrister, later of Mount Falcon, Tipperary. Johnson wrote her several affectionate letters, one of which is quoted in Hunter's memoirs; he gives no date, but it was evidently written not long after her arrival in Ireland and some time before the winter, so she probably left England in the summer of 1758. "You have gone at the worst time; the splendor of Dublin is only to be seen in a Parliament winter," wrote Johnson, ". . . I shall be glad to hear from you the history of your management; whether you have a house or shop, and what companions you have found; let me know every good and every evil that befalls you."

It is fair to conclude that she did not leave England without the advice and encouragement of Smart's family and friends. It is not fair to say with Mr Brittain that "she decided to remain no longer on a sinking ship," and to suggest that she tried "to get as far away from her husband as she could." We do not know what dangers and hardships may have been looming up before her in England; she had in any case to accept Newbery's offer to make her living, and it is quite likely that Marianne Falkiner asked her to come and stay.[1]

[1] Marianne is the sister whom Smart recalls so vividly in his poem *The Hop Garden*.

No, the strange thing—at this point, anyway—is not Nancy's neglect of Kit, but Kit's apparent neglect of Nancy. It is not till quite a long time later that he begins to complain bitterly: "they have separated me and my bosom." Perhaps he was just expecting her return in the ordinary course of things, or perhaps—and one cannot help feeling this is more likely—he was going about in a sort of dream all those months, brooding over his great liturgical project. Anyway, this opening section (Fragment A) of *Jubilate Agno* is all we have to tell us what was going on in his mind during the first half of 1759.

It was certainly under composition at this time, for the next known section (Fragment B) was begun before August, and in between A and B (which were marked by Smart folios 1 and 3) there was another folio (2) which is now missing; it would have contained another hundred "Let" versicles; moreover the "For" responses which should have accompanied all these versicles (about 200 of them) are also missing. It cannot be far wrong, then, to assign Fragment A (folio 1) to the early part of 1759. It is all we have to show us the plan in Smart's mind before he abandoned it, It begins:

Rejoice in God, O ye tongues; give the glory to the Lord and the Lamb.
Nations, and languages, and every Creature, in which is the breath of Life.
Let man and beast appear before him, and magnify his name together.
Let Noah and his company approach the throne of Grace, and do homage to the Ark of their Salvation
Let Abraham present a Ram, and worship the God of his Redemption.
Let Isaac, the Bridegroom, kneel with his Camels, and bless the hope of his pilgrimage.
Let Jacob and his speckled Drove adore the good Shepherd of Israel.

There follows name after name from the Old Testament, each with an appropriate animal—beast, bird, reptile, or insect. The opening is conceived after the Order for Morning Prayer. But also there is an echo of the adoration of the Lamb in the *Apocalypse*, vii, 9–10.

There were two chief novelties that Smart wanted to introduce into the liturgy. The first was to change the words of the Old Testament so as to show their fulfilment by Christ in the New; the introduction of "the Lamb" into the opening psalm of Morning Prayer is an indication of his intention. It may seem a small point but to Smart it was of great importance both morally and doctrinally. Morally, he thought there was great danger in the hatreds and angers narrated in the Old Testament being taken as examples of conduct. This way of treating the Old Testament is at least as old as the Alexandrine Fathers—and Gregory of Nyssa, who interprets the Psalmist's enemies as his own evil inclinations (see page 149). Nor was it a new idea to Smart; he had held it at least as long ago as 1750 when he wrote his poem supporting Dr Webster against Warburton.[1] Later on, as will be seen, he put it into practice wholesale, changing cruelty to mercy and revenge into reconciliation in his metric version of the psalms. Doctrinally, too, he thought it was of importance; people did not realize sufficiently that from the great Old Testament figures (especially David), if they were presented properly, we could get a wonderful likeness of Christ; moreover, there were many passages of shining beauty about natural things which were really meant to describe Christ. His idea of Christ, the Word, as not only a man but a universal force holding together all the levels of creation, was responsible for his second and more alarming novelty.

He never wanted to be anything but an orthodox Christian. But he could not resist the conviction, which had been latent

[1]   Great MOSES led away his chosen band;
    When ISRAEL'S host with all their stores,
    Passed thro' the ruby-tinctur'd crystal shores,
The wilderness of waters and of land . . .

    The legislator held the scythe of fate,
      Where'er his legions chanc'd to stray,
      Death and destruction mark'd their bloody way;
Immoderate was their rage, for mortal was their hate.

    But when the king of righteousness arose,
      And on the illumin'd East serenely smil'd,
    He shone with meekest mercy on his foes,
      Bright as the sun, but as the moon-beams mild;
        From anger, fell revenge, and discord free,
        He bad war's hellish clangour cease,
        In pastoral simplicity and peace,
And show'd to man that face, which MOSES could not see.

within him all his life, that Christ represented not only all men but the whole of creation; the Church that he founded must be the Church of all creation. There was no hope of man getting in touch with the Angels—with the Cherubim and the Seraphim, with the Thrones and the Powers and the Dominations—unless he were also in touch with the birds and beasts, the fishes and insects, the flowers and herbs, and all the manifestations of the four elements. Very early he indicated this belief by deliberately confusing the word "Ark"; the priestly Ark of the Covenant and the seaborne Ark of Noah were both for him one image of the true Church.

> Let the Levites of the Lord take the Beavers of ye brook alive into the Ark of the Testimony.

There follows a list of Levites, each with an animal, some clean and some unclean. It is a pity the "For" responses are all missing; they might have made these "Let" versicles less odd and more applicable to church worship.

The second of Smart's novelties was the more eccentric; but the first may well have been more dangerous; for it was an old charge against Roman Catholics that they feared the strong meat of the Old Testament and hashed it up only as a setting for the New. Rome was the last place where Smart was intending to go; his aim was to universalize the Church of *England* to take the place of Rome. But if Wesley's innovations could be seriously suspected, as they were, of being Romish, how much more Smart's with his Popish wife and his Popish devotion to the Saints and prayers for the dead. Moreover he made extensive use of the Apocrypha, or deutero-canonical books of the Bible, which were recognized as equally inspired with the others by the Church of Rome but not by the Church of England; indeed there were periodical movements within the Church of England to have these books banned.

There is no information at this time of any alarm about Smart's Protestant orthodoxy (though there are distinct hints of it later on in 1763), but alarm there must have been if he went on solemnly outlining his plans to friends and visitors. It was not enough that he had stopped his uproarious public prayers. These liturgical innovations were an even more urgent reason for persuading him to go quietly out of circulation.

We come again and again to the same question. Was Smart really insane?

Without even attempting as yet to answer the question, it must be said that this Fragment A (113 versicles in all) bears absolutely no signs of "chaotic discontinuation of thought." On the contrary, there is ample evidence of very calm and closely-wrought thinking. Since that seems to be now the prevailing opinion, I only will give one or two examples which have passed unnoticed by editors and commentators, I think, because they have not noticed the extensive use Smart made of the Apocrypha or deutero-canonical books.

For example, the first allusion to "jeopardy," an important word for Smart which he appropriated, is concealed in this versicle:

Let Savaran bless with the Elephant, who gave his life for his country that he might put on immortality.

Mr Bond comments that "*Savaran* is not a Biblical name" and that he can find no explanation for its intrusion. But it occurs (though it may well be a textual error) in the deutero-canonical book of *Maccabees* (I, vi, 43–6) where it is related how "Eleazar *surnamed* Savaran" slew the elephant from beneath and was entombed in its fall: "Eleazar also, *surnamed* Savaran, . . . put himself in jeopardy, to the end he might deliver his people and get himself a perpetual name."

Another versicle, which has something of the appeal of a cryptogram, is based on an apocryphal book:

Let Manasses bless with the Wild-Ass—liberty begetteth insolence, but necessity is the mother of prayer.

Manasses is the king Manasseh whose sins and subsequent humiliation are recorded in *Kings* and *Chronicles*; but the main reference to his repentance and prayer, with the Greek form of his name, is the Apocryphal "Prayer of Manasses, King of Judah, when he was holden captive in Babylon." But we have still not caught up with the Wild Ass. He is found in *Jeremiah*, ii, 23, and xix, 5, where the prophet denounces the burning of children in honour of Baal—which was in fact the special sin of Manasseh. Jeremy says it took place in the valley of the sons of Hinnom and likens its practitioners to the Wild Ass scenting its mate. The wild ass is a type of insolent liberty (*Job*, xxxix, 5), but also of humiliation as in *Hosea* (viii, 8), where the captive Israelites "are gone up to Assyria, a wild ass alone by himself." Thus there were no less than seven references interwoven in Smart's head when he wrote this verse: a remarkable achievement even allowing for eighteenth-century familiarity with the Bible.

By contrast the versicle which conceals a reference to the black Africans is plain and comfortable:

> Let Ebed-Melech bless with the Mantiger, the blood of the Lord is sufficient to do away the offence of Cain, and reinstate the creature which is amerced.

Ebed-Melech is the good Ethiopian who saved the life of Jeremiah (xxxviii and xxxix) and was promised salvation by the Lord. The Mantichora is one of Pliny's strange animals which found its way into all the mediaeval bestiaries as the Mantiger. The bestiaries discover it in various places, but Pliny put it in Ethiopia: "Ctesias writeth that in Aethiopia likewise there is a beast which he calleth Mantichora." (*Plinie's Naturall Historie*, Eighth Booke, Ch. xxi, tr. Holland, 1601, p. 206.) The belief in the Curse of Cain, which has dwindled now to South Africa, was generally held in Smart's day, but he says it was lifted by the promise of the Redeemer.

Another phrase from the "apocryphal" books, though very slight in the text, became extremely fecund in Smart's imagination later. He has this straightforward verse about Tobias and his dog:

> Let Tobias bless Charity with his Dog, who is faithful, vigilant, and a friend in poverty.

followed by this:

> Let Anna bless God with the Cat, who is worthy to be presented before the throne of grace, when he has trampled upon the idol in his prank.

Mr Bond comments rightly that this would be the Anna who was Tobias's mother, but he adds that the cat is "non-Biblical." Not so. In the beautiful book of *Baruch* (vi, 22) there is a mocking description of the Babylonian idols which has this verse:

> Upon their bodies and heads sit bats, swallows, and birds, and the cats also.

On the strength of these last three words about the cats' contempt for idols Smart christianized all cats, especially his own Jeoffry, and was able to dedicate to God with the utmost delight all their beautifully controlled activities.

This is the old whimsical Smart peeping through the grave and chosen words of his liturgical experiment. Before long he had abandoned it as such, or at least was planning to turn it into ordinary verse and have it set to music:

> Let Jubal rejoice with Cæcilia, the woman and the slow-worm praise the name of the Lord.
> For I pray the Lord Jesus to translate my MAGNIFICAT into verse and represent it.

By the time he wrote those lines—in July or August of this year—he was keeping up *Jubilate Agno* only as a kind of spiritual diary. Another crisis in his affairs, bringing with it a deep spiritual crisis in his soul, was upon him. The next fragment, which has survived with its "For" verses, begins:

> Let Elizur rejoice with the Partridge,[1] who is a prisoner of state and is proud of his keepers.
> For I am not without authority in my jeopardy, which I derive inevitably from the glory of the name of the Lord.

Disputes were going on in the wider circle of his relatives about whether and how he should be put away, and he himself was preparing for a new stage in his "jeopardy"; he was bracing himself to accept external humiliations in the trust that they would lead him further into the Kingdom of God within.

[1] The "Partridge" seems to be a wry reminiscence of the caged quail in his own fable of 1755, which happened to have been published about the time he regained his liberty, in the *Gentleman's Magazine* of December, 1758—no doubt as a help to raising money. See A. Sherbo, *Notes and Queries*, February, 1955 (p. 65).

Let Zohar rejoice with Cychramus who cometh with the quails on a particular affair.

For there is a traveling for the glory of God without going to Italy or France.

Let Magdiel rejoice with Ascarides, which is the life of the bowels—the worm hath a part in our frame.

For I rejoice like a worm in the rain in him that cherishes and from him that tramples . . .

For I am ready for the trumpet & alarm to fight, to die & to rise again.

All the first 120 versicles and their responses of this fragment (BI) sway in movement and counter-movement: ironic resignation to his fate which changes sometimes to a tone of undisguised bitterness; and, on the other hand, a humble resignation which rises to a note of jubilant courage in the service of Christ—"For I have adventured myself in the name of the Lord, and he hath marked me for his own."

In the beginning there are disjointed hints of a meeting and disputes at Canonbury House, while Smart, indifferent to what is going on, plays with his daughters Polly and Bess, aged six and five respectively.

For I meditate the peace of Europe amongst family bickerings and domestic jars . . .

For I bless God in the rising generation which is on my side.

Let Ephah rejoice with Buprestis, the Lord endue us with temperance & humanity, till every cow have her mate!

For I am come home again, but there is nobody to kill the calf or to pay the musick.

Smart's bitterness seems to have been chiefly aroused by his more distant relatives: Francis Smart of Snotterton, whose heir-at-law he was, and Richard Smart, a London lawyer, some sort of second-cousin. Frank Smart had just mortgaged the ancestral estate for three or four thousand pounds, and was planning to cut Christopher out of his will in favour of Richard Smart. Christopher seems to have been persuaded finally to sign some sort of renunciation on condition that his mother was looked after. The climax came on 13 August when he repeats three times: "For this day I made over my inheritance to my mother in consideration of her infirmities," "in consideration of her age," "in consideration of her poverty." There follows three more verses in which he repeats, "For I bless the thirteenth of August in which I had the grace to obey the voice of Christ in my conscience," "in which I was willing to run all hazards for the sake of the name of the Lord," "in which I was willing to be called a fool for the sake of Christ."[1]

But the six animals in the "Let" invocations which accompany these six verses give terrible hints of the depths to which the quarrel descended. Mr Bond writes of them:

> The undercurrent of bitterness in this part of the poem here rises to a climax, where in succeeding lines the Stag (horns), Kite, Wittol (cuckold), Locust, Woodcock and Gull are associated with Smart's renunciation of his birthright . . . and the theme of cuckoldry recurs explicitly or implicitly . . . elsewhere.

For example:

> For they throw my horns in my face and reptiles made themselves wings against me. (115)

Yet he claimed that his renunciation was for spiritual motives:

> For my grounds in New Canaan shall infinitely compensate for the flats & maynes of Staindrop Moor.

What poor Anna-Maria thought or said or did about the false and disgusting hints against her fidelity we do not know. Smart's bitterness seems all against his cousins (whom I take to be his "brethren") not against his wife. He says of them:

> For my brethren have dealt deceitfully as a brook, and as the stream of brooks that pass away. (74)

Whereas in the same place he speaks of his wife and children with wistful affection; the invocation of Abigail, David's wife, suggests to him:

> For the Fatherless Children and widows are never deserted of the Lord. (70)

[1] For a full discussion of Smart's "inheritance" see the end of Chapter Thirteen.

For I bless God for my retreat at CANBURY, as it was the place of the nativity of my children. (75)

For I pray God to give them the food which I cannot earn for them otherwise than by prayer. (76)

But his attitude is strangely listless and detached. "At least," he seems to be saying, "I have my cat, Jeoffrey!"

For I am possessed of a cat, surpassing in beauty, from whom I take occasion to bless Almighty God. (68)

There is no doubt that Christopher's preoccupation at this time was chiefly with himself; he saw himself as a knight in shining armour off on a lone quest to find the Holy Grail. How far this bright image of himself was a delusion or a true incentive to a higher state of life it is impossible to say. The struggle before him was formidable enough in all conscience. The invocation of Ruth the Moabitess reminds him of the Roman Catholic Nancy and how, with her gone, he must live in complete continence:

For I am in charity with the French who are my foes and Moabites because of the Moabitish woman. (56)

For my Angel is always ready at a pinch to help me out and keep me up. (57)

For Agricola is SAINT GEORGE, but his son CHRISTOPHER must slay the Dragon with a PHEON's head. (58)

For they have seperated me and my bosom, whereas the right comes by setting us together. (59)

The Agricola-Georgos equation begins a sort of Arthurian fantasy more developed later on. The "Pheon" is the arrow or spearhead in the Smart coat-of-arms. The "Dragon" is lust. Henceforth he and his wife will be joined only in a spiritual marriage:

For the Sun's at work to make me a garment & the Moon is at work for my wife. (111)

Here, at the ending of this chapter, something must be stressed which may not yet have been sufficiently brought out; Smart's entry into the asylum, even if it was physically compelled, was a voluntary consecration of himself to God. Professors Ainsworth and Noyes have already pointed out that the text of *Jubilate Agno* seems to show that Smart made a vow of chastity. But the text is equally clear about other aspects of his dedication. It seems that he made his own version of all the three monastic vows—poverty, chastity and obedience—which were the Early Church's interpretation of Christ's counsels of perfection.

His obedience admittedly was quite individual; it was not obedience to any rule, it was "to obey the voice of Christ in my conscience"; but it was conceived in imitation of Christ who, as St Paul says, "was obedient unto death," and by obedience unto temporal death destroyed the spiritual death which came by disobedience.

The co-ordination in Smart's three eccentric vows is made clear by an otherwise mysterious passage, written later on, about conquering three things—"the coffin, the cradle, and the purse." As will be seen in the next chapter, where this passage is quoted, "the coffin" signifies "death by disobedience" as the cradle signifies weakness of the flesh and the purse love of money. A scriptural co-ordination of the three could also be St John's "the lust of the flesh, the lust of the eyes and the pride of life."

Meanwhile here are three verses (there are many others) which show the scope of Smart's voluntary dedication to poverty, chastity and obedience.

Poverty: "For tis no more a merit to provide for oneself, but to quit all for the sake of the Lord." (81)
Chastity: "For beauty is better to look upon than to meddle with and tis good for a man not to know a woman." (104)
Obedience: "For I am ready to die for his sake—who lay down his life for all mankind." (98)

A last, spasmodic outbreak of public prayer—occasioned no doubt by all this controversy and suppressed fervour—followed by another bout of fever seems to have led up to his actual confinement:

For I blessed God in St James's Park till I routed all the company. (89)

For the officers of the peace are at variance with me, and the watchman smites me with his staff. (90)

For they lay wagers touching my life.—God be gracious to the winners. (92)

114

For the piety of Rizpah is imitable in the Lord—wherefore I pray
for the dead. (93).

In contrast with these odd mutterings is a sudden passage
filled to the brim with limpid self-knowledge, one of the
sweetest, the most luminous, the best-worded of all his
verses:

> Let Hushim rejoice with the King's Fisher, who is of royal beauty,
> tho' plebeian size.
> For in my nature I quested for beauty, but God, God hath sent
> me to sea for pearls. (30)

Sometimes in the transformation of Smart the scribbler
into Smart the man-of-prayer, we seem to be on the brink of
a great conversion story. But the look on that face before it
disappears into the private asylum is hard to decipher. Is it
the blank but flickering leer of the psychotic? Or is it the
rapt, wounded longing of the natural contemplative?

Dr Battie would have said that the two were precisely the
same. But Dr Battie, wise in his own generation, was in the
longer view mistaken.

NINE

❖

"At Chelsey or Elsewhere"

CHARLES BURNEY, one of Smart's earliest friends, had
been in Norfolk for his health for the past nine years; but
early in 1760 he returned to London with his family and
settled in Poland Street. He went to see Johnson to inquire
about Kit. Mrs Thrale gives the conversation as repeated to
her by Burney, though at a very much later date (1777):[1]

> BURNEY: I vex to hear of poor Kit's going to Chelsey—
> JOHNSON: But a madman must be confined, sir, at Chelsey or elsewhere.

There followed Johnson's heartless remarks about the ale-
house and no man needing exercise for his health. The conversation took place, Mrs Thrale recalls, when Smart had
not been long put into private lodgings. It is in complete
contrast with Johnson's later views recorded by Boswell
under 1763: "I did not think he ought to be shut up. His
infirmities were not noxious to society." This illustrates how
impossible it is for us to be certain about Smart's sanity or
insanity. If modern doctors can fail to agree about a patient
actually under observation, how can we, at two hundred
years' distance, pronounce on a case about which a contemporary observer like Johnson could be in two minds?

But what is more immediately interesting is the mention
of Chelsea. Hitherto all writers on Smart have said that there
is no clue as to the place of his second confinement. But here
is a clue as large as life—if Mrs Thrale and Charles Burney's

---

[1] *Thraliana*, ed. Balderston, Oxford 1951, vol. I, p. 176.

memories are to be trusted. There was only one private mad-house known to have existed in Chelsea before 1774. That was Turlington's House, better known as Shrewsbury House, the old town residence of the Talbots. "A spacious house with a spacious garden," it was situated where Cheyne Walk backs on Cheyne Row, facing the Thames. From 1757 to 1766 it was leased by a Mr Robert Turlington who ran it as a private madhouse, though he left the management almost entirely to a man called King.

Unfortunately no record was kept of its inmates; it ter-minated its career before the law about keeping records was put into force; and both Smart's confinement and his release were so informal, it is most unlikely that any kind of written confirmation will ever turn up that he was lodged in Turling-ton's House.

Our only information about it comes from the House of Commons Inquiry into private madhouses in January 1763—which, in fact, was directed almost exclusively against Tur-lington and King. This information, such as it is, agrees with what details are known of Smart's confinement, and it is safe to say that if he was not in Turlington House, he was in some place very like it.

It did not cater expressly for lunatics, but for persons who for some reason or other (drunkenness, for example) were unable to look after themselves, and whose relatives were prepared to pay to have them kept in strict seclusion. Diet and apparel were according to the rates paid, which varied between twenty and sixty pounds a year. Free movement was allowed about the house and in the garden. Chains were never used. Pen and paper were allowed, except for letters to persons outside.

The other side of the picture is presented in an article in the *Gentleman's Magazine* of January 1763, occasioned obviously by the House of Commons inquiry. (It is highly probable that this article, and perhaps the inquiry also, had a good deal to do with Smart's eventual release.)

When a person is forcibly taken or artfully decoyed into a private madhouse, he is, without any authority or any further charge, than that of an impatient heir, a mercenary relation, or a pretended friend, instantly seized upon by a set of inhuman ruffians trained up to this barbarous profession, stripped naked, and conveyed to a dark-room. If the patient complains, the attendant brutishly orders him not to rave, calls for assistants, and ties him down to a bed, from which he is not released until he submits to their pleasure. Next morning, a doctor is gravely introduced who, taking the report of the keeper, pronounces the unfortunate person a lunatic, and declares that he must be reduced by physic. If the revolted victim offers to argue against it by alleging any proofs of sanity, a motion is made by the waiter for the doctor to withdraw, and if the patient, or rather the prisoner, persists in vindicating his reason, or refuses to take the dose, he is then deemed raving mad; the banditti of the whole house are called in, the forcing instruments are brought, upon which the sensible patient must submit to take whatever is administered. When the poor patient thus finds himself deprived of all communication with the world, and denied the use of pen and paper, all he can do is to compose himself under the unhappy situation in the hope of a more favourable report. But any composure under such affliction is immediately deemed a melancholy or sulky fit by the waiter who reports it as such to the doctor in the hearing of the despairing prisoner, whose misery is thus redoubled in finding that the doctor prescribed a repetition of the dose, and that from day to day, until the patient is so debilitated in body that in time it impairs his mind.[1]

This circumstantial account may well be true of the established private madhouses which kept a doctor in attendance and professed to cure lunacy by the usual brutal methods; it may actually refer to Miles's House in Hoxton, which was the only other house beside Turlington's brought into the very limited House of Commons inquiry. But its details sound too harsh and systematic for the more easy-going house in Chelsea. What is probably true in general, however, is that the inmate on first arriving was given a cruel "working-over" to convince him of the advisability of docile submission.

That was evidently poor Smart's experience. The first certain indication that he was actually inside one of these houses comes in these soul-chilling lines written about 1 September 1759:

LET PETER rejoice with the MOON FISH who keeps up his life in the waters by night.

FOR I pray the Lord JESUS that cured the LUNATICK to be merciful to all my brethren and sisters in these houses.

[1] Quoted from Jones, *Lunacy, Law and Conscience* (1955), p. 32.

Let Andrew rejoice with the Whale, who is arrayd in beauteous blue
& is combination of bulk & activity.

For they work me with their harping-irons, which is a barbarous
instrument, because I am more unguarded than others. (B1 123-4)

This is the beginning of a series of New Testament invocations; there is a gap in the manuscript between the Old
and the New. It will be observed how Smart's personal
references are subordinate to his invocations; the apostles
suggest fish; the whale, harpoons; harpoons, harping-irons—
"the forcing instruments," perhaps, of the article just quoted.

But these are Smart's only references to ill-treatment. Very
soon there are signs of a better state of affairs:

Let Sadoc rejoice with the Bleak, who playeth upon the surface in
the Sun.

For I bless God that I am not in a dungeon, but am allowed the light
of the Sun. (148)

He was allowed pen and an abundance of paper; he had his
beautiful Jeoffrey—who must by now be one of the famous
cats of history;[1] he had, later on at any rate, a little garden of
his own where he grew carnations, and this was the subject
of several joyful entries. He had privacy, but was not kept
solitary; Mrs Thrale says that he taught Latin to the children
of the keeper, and was paid for it. It is Mrs Thrale also who
says: "The famous Christopher Smart, who was both a wit
and a scholar and *visited as such* while under confinement..."
(italics mine); but these visits probably did not begin till
1762, and may have followed on a law-suit *Rex v. Turlington*
(1761) mentioned in the next chapter.

But if Smart's three-and-a-half years' confinement was by
no means one long misery, the reason was mainly to be found
within himself. He had entered, if not voluntarily, at least
with full knowledge and resignation. He was determined to
make of it a purifying experience which should raise him
nearer to God. Most of all, he was liable to be lifted up occasionally by a sublime joy in the smallest sights and sounds of

[1] The long and delightful passage on Jeoffrey is probably now familiar
to many readers from Dame Edith Sitwell's *Atlantic* anthology (I, p.
541); it was earlier printed in Auden and Pearson's *Poets of the English
Language*.

his fellow-creatures—especially when they praised their Creator with a sort of faint refraction of the Divine Intelligence. Some of these stored moments of happiness burst out and flowered later on in some of the lovely stanzas of *A Song to David*:

> For ADORATION, beyond match,
> The scholar bulfinch aims to catch
>   The soft flute's iv'ry touch;
> And, careless, on the hazel spray,
> The daring redbreast keeps at bay
>   The damsel's greedy clutch . . .

> For ADORATION, in the dome
> Of CHRIST, the sparrow's find an home,
>   And on his olives perch:
> The swallow also dwells with thee,
> O man of God's humility,
>   Within his Savour CHURCH.

The moments of joy and clarity in *Jubilate Agno* (Fragments B1 and B2 of which take us continuously to about August 1760)[1] are, unfortunately, outnumbered by the passages of dark unintelligibility. The dissociation between the "Let" invocations and the "For" responses becomes almost complete.

There is one dark passage, however, about "the coffin, the cradle and the purse," which it is important to elucidate if possible. The editors note the passage as unexplained, but it yields to understanding if one accepts (as outlined in the previous chapter) that Smart undertook his own version of the monastic vows of poverty, chastity and obedience. Here is the passage:

> For the coffin and the cradle and the purse are all against a man.
> For the coffin is for the dead and death came by disobedience.
> For the cradle is for weakness and the child of man was originally strong from ye womb.
> For the purse is for money and money is dead matter with the stamp of human vanity.
> For the adversary frequently sends these particular images out of the fire to those whom they concern.
> For the coffin is for me because I have nothing to do with it.

[1] Mr Bond numbers them continuously; but the "Let" versicles are missing in B2.

> For the cradle is for me because the old Dragon attacked me in it
> I overcame in Christ.
> For the purse is for me because I have neither money nor human
> friends (276–83).

To trample on the coffin (as Christ does in old pictures of
the Resurrection) is to conquer death by accepting obedience.
To reject the purse is to embrace voluntary poverty. The
cradle is that weakness of the flesh, the loss of integrity, which
came with Original Sin. Mr Stead explains the cradle as a
reference to Smart's ill-health in infancy. That, too, may be
implied; but the key reference is to the Woman and Child
attacked by the Dragon in *Revelation* xii, and the Dragon is
for Smart particularly the horned dragon of lust, already
mentioned in verse 58.

These lines were written in December 1759. The lengthen-
ing winter nights were a bad time for Smart:

> For the devil hath most power in winter, because darkness pre-
> vails. (296)
> For the more the light is defective, the more the powers of dark-
> ness prevail. (315)

This symbolic darkness brings home to us how terribly alone
Smart was in his spiritual adventure. He was doing the sort
of thing that Catholic saints have done, but without any of the
aids of that Church, and, on his part, without any sympathy
for it. He was determined that the Church of England was a
branch of the true Church, and, further, that it should be
the main branch in Europe:

> For I bless God that the CHURCH of ENGLAND is one of the
> SEVEN evn the candlestick of the Lord (126–7)
> For the ENGLISH TONGUE shall be the language of the WEST.

To this religious patriotism the Seven Years War added a
note of belligerent nationalism which had hitherto been quite
foreign to him:

> For I prophecy that the exactions of Moab will soon be at an end.
> For the Moabites even the French are in their chastisement for
> humiliation.
> For I prophecy that the Reformation will make way in France when
> Moab is made meek by being well drubbed by the English . . .

> For the Liturgy will obtain in all languages.
> For England is the head and not the tail.
> For England is the head of Europe in the spirit.
>
> (C.95–102)

Smart never shows any sign of being in touch with the reality of the Church of England as it was under Archbishops Potter, Herring and Secker. It is no wonder that, being completely without any form of spiritual guidance, he should have wandered into some rather murky by-paths.

> For CHASTITY is the key of knowledge as in Esdras, Sr Isaac Newton & now, God be praised, in me.
> For Newton nevertheless is more of error than of the truth, but I am of the WORD of GOD. (B.194–5)

This is not a safe way of regarding chastity; it is not surprising to find Smart in Fragment C (written between March and May 1761) falling into the old error of equating chastity with misogyny. It is true that this error has appeared to prevail at some periods in the Church, but it was never orthodox; it is not a sign of grace, it is Catharism. A denunciation of women leads Smart into one of the most shockingly crazy of his passages, about horns; it goes on for thirty-five verses till the manuscript is broken off. A few lines here will be more than enough:

> For the horn on the forehead is a tower upon an arch.
> For it is a strong munition against the adversary, who is sickness & death.
> For it is instrumental in subjecting the woman.
> For the insolence of the woman has increased ever since Man has been crest-fallen.
> For they have turned the horn into scoff and derision without ceasing.
> For we are amerced of God, who has his horn . . . (C.138–44)

Another of Smart's crazes concerns the word "bull":

> For BULL in the first place is the word of Almighty God.
> For he is a creature of infinite magnitude in the height.
>
> (B.676–7)

There follows a long list of creatures and elements that come "under Bull." It does not seem to be the bull of the zodiac. Smart seems to have in mind the Mithraic conception of the blood and seed of a sacrificed bull giving new life to the world.

This in turn appears to have descended from the older fertility rite—preserved till modern times among some African peoples—by which the king or chief ensured the harvest by a ceremonial act and had to be killed when he became impotent. There are some who hold that a form of this cult persisted underground during the Middle Ages and that it entered into the ritual of the Cathars and even of the Templars. There are some also who say that there are traces of its symbolism in early Freemasonry in the form of an attachment to the House of Stuart—or perhaps of a regret at having had to kill King Charles. I am here on ground that is quite foreign to me; but, for a reason to be given in a moment, I think it worth noting that Smart was apparently an "accepted MASON"[1] (B.199) and that he does (B.70, 274, D.206) develop a sympathy for the House of Stuart which was not apparent before, especially for Charles I "By marriage ill-advised akin To Moab and the man of sin!"

Also to be noted is his strange search for what I have called "spiritual credentials," his claimed descent from "Becket" and from "the steward of the island":

> For I am redoubted, and redoubtable in the Lord, as is THOMAS
> BECKET my father (B.134; see also B.434)
> For I am descended from the steward of the island blessed be the
> name of the Lord Jesus king of England. (B.137)

The reason why all these odd and disparate facts have been noted is that it is possible to find them united in a sinister pattern. All of them—horns, bull, king-killing, Cathars, and the grail element in the "steward of the island" are gathered together in *The Arrow and the Sword* by Mr Hugh Ross Williamson, which develops the so-called "conventional" theory that St Thomas Becket was a leading Cathar whose death was "the ritual killing of the Divine King in the witch-cult." I do not, naturally, hold this theory myself, but suppose it possible that in some form or other it may have been floating about in Smart's day.

---

[1] By courtesy of the Archivist of the Grand Lodge Library, I am informed that Smart's name is not on the list of the Ancients (compiled between 1751 and 1768), but that his membership of the Craft is generally accepted.

"The steward of the island" is Agricola, name of the Roman general in Britain, whom Smart identifies with St George. Apart from the feeble play on words (both the names mean "farmer"), there may be a Grail or Arthurian background. St George, in the *Faerie Queene*, plays the part of Perceval or Galahad. In some Welsh genealogies going back to Roman Britain, Aircol (i.e. Agricola) the Long-handed, is given, some time before Gildas, as Protector of Demetia (i.e. Dyfed in south-west Wales)—where, it is said, the Grail romance originated. "Dr J. L. Weston has established that the original stories which developed into the Arthurian romance—those of *Perceval* and *Gawain*—had their rise in precisely those regions where Mithraic remains are known to exist. She has identified the original author, Bleheris, with Bledri, the son of . . . Cadivor, Prince of Dyfed, the Pembrokeshire peninsula of Wales" (*The Arrow and the Sword*, pp. 54, 113). Kindred fancies are the Judaic descent of the British and the Romans, and that Christ and some Apostles were present at Glastonbury and in those parts:

Paul & Tychicus were in England with Agricola my father . . .
The Lord was at Glastonbury in yᵉ body and blessed the thorn . ..
The Lord was at Bristol & blessed the waters there . . .
The waters of Bath were blessed by Sᵗ Matthias. (B.231–4)

These are harmless and indeed traditional fancies—though they had in the past been used as a backstairs way of claiming hieratic power independent of the clergy. Perhaps a more sinister interpretation could be put on Smart's repeated praise of dancing and "the Dance," while at the same time he violently condemns painting and sculpture:

For Painting is a species of idolatry, tho' not so gross as statuary.
(B.673)

It is certain that Smart, like most scholars of his day, did have some acquaintance with occult lore, for example:

For Preferment is not from the East, West or South, but from the North, where Satan has most power. (B.422)

On the other hand, he recoils in horror from black magic

B.300)—and also from homosexuality (B.419), which was closely associated with it by public opinion in former times.

Personally I am convinced that there is no sinister pattern to be found in Smart's aberrations. They are the dead-ends of trains of thought suggested by his wide reading and then found to be unprofitable. (These fragments B and C were not meant for publication.) Frequently they are contradicted either in the text itself or shortly afterwards. For example, the denunciation of painting and sculpture does not come from the real Smart; a year or two later he is enthusiastically praising Roubillac and Romney. Again—and closer to the point—his fulminations against women and his unfounded suspicions of his wife are contradicted or at least softened by several loving references in the same passage which ends with the extravaganza about "horns":

> Let Miamin rejoice with Mezereon. God be gracious to Polly and Bess and all Canbury. (C.73)
> Let Palal rejoice with the female Balsamime. God be gracious to my wife. (C.108)

And the name Tabbaoth (Hebrew for "rings") suggests the flower Goldy Locks and "the lass with the golden locks":

> Let Tabbaoth rejoice with Goldy Locks. God be merciful to my wife. (C.128)

When one remembers, once again, how much an imaginative man shut up within himself is at the mercy of his own thoughts, it is astonishing that Smart retained so much of sweetness and sanity in his general outlook.

Yet, while Smart must be firmly acquitted of any kind of conscious heterodoxy, his aberrations do remain disquieting symptoms of a mental or spiritual maladjustment still persisting and gone to ground. They are the shadows spoken of at the end of Chapter Six. One cannot ignore that the reminiscences of wife and children just quoted are ushered in by a long series of names from the tenth chapter of the Book of Ezra. It is a list of all those who were gathered together by Ezra in the pouring rain and obliged to drive away their heathen wives, Moabites, Ammonites, Amorrhites, etc., and the children born of them. (Smart uses the

Septuagint form "Esdras" for "Ezra"; he also mentions the purifying effects of rain several times in this passage.) Now Esdras, or Ezra, was one of Smart's greatest Old Testament heroes, second only perhaps to David.

> For CHASTITY is the key of knowledge as in Esdras . . . & now, God be praised, in me. (B.194)

I think there is little doubt that Smart abandoned his wife and children, violating his own tenderest feelings, because he thought he was called by the Lord to be a prophet who should reform the Church of England. It had been an enforced separation at first, when he was obliged to go into confinement, but in his brooding he came to see the hand of the Lord in it—or to make a virtue of necessity—because she was a "Moabitish woman." Hence his spasms of bitterness against women in general, his apocalyptic anti-Romanism, his crazy search for spiritual credentials: all symptoms of this clotted, stock pseudo-messianic obsession which he could conceal but did not know how to get rid of.

Another example of his depression comes in the dark December of 1759. His entries in *Jubilate Agno* have tailed off into a mere list of New Testament characters with a fish attached to each. But every now and again comes the explosion of some deep and rankling grievance, sometimes touched off by a verbal resemblance, sometimes unheralded:

> Let Claudia rejoice with Pascer—the purest creatures minister to wantonness by unthankfulness . . .
> Let Zenas rejoice with Pecten—the Lord obliterate the laws of man!
> Let Philemon rejoice with Pelagia—The laws & judgement are impudence & blindness . . .
> Let Antipas rejoice with Pentadactylus—A papist hath no sentiment God bless CHURCHILL.

This ends the fragment known as B1. I think all these outbursts have to do with his wife, culminating in the curious intrusion of Churchill. Charles Churchill's earlier career was ruined by his unfortunate marriage; his acquaintance with Smart is proved by subsequent events mentioned in the next chapter. It looks as if Smart had been swept by a momentary irrational wave of sympathy with him in revulsion against women in general, and his wife and her religion in particular.

But fortunately there were many moments when he forgot himself and his delusion and remembered only to praise God.

> For the blessing of God upon the grass is in shades of Green visible to a nice observer as they light upon the surface of the earth. (B.670)

There are moments also when it is clear that his thought and his learning, though perhaps fragmentary, were by no means shallow. What is the explanation, for example, of this strange passage?

> For there is a blessing from the STONE of Jesus which is founded upon hell to the precious jewell on the right hand of God. (B.31)

There is only one possible explanation and it is to be found in the teachings of the Greek fathers, Origen and Gregory of Nyssa. They believed in the "apokatastasis," the restoration of all creatures, in which the flames of hell would eventually be purified; this thought of the basic continuity between heaven and hell is one to which Smart recurs several times. "The precious jewel on the right hand of God" is the "eikon" or resemblance to God which is restored to man when his sins are cleansed. St Gregory likens it to the ring which the Father gave to the Prodigal Son: "The ring on his hand, because of the carved stone, signifies the regaining of the Image."[1]

Here is the explanation of the line in stanza 30 of *A Song to David*, which would otherwise not be intelligible:

> His WORD accomplished the design,
> From brightest gem to deepest mine.

The deepest mine is the stone of hell, and the brightest gem is the jewel on the right hand.

After the end of Fragment C (May 1761) there comes a long gap of more than a year. Fragment D, the last surviving section, begins in July 1762 and goes on to the end of January 1763, the very eve of his release.

[1] *St Gregory of Nyssa: The Lord's Prayer*, tr. Hilda Graef (London, 1954), p. 41.

TEN

Release

I N Fragment D *Jubilate Agno* takes on a shape completely
different from both the liturgical solemnity of A and the
chaotic spiritual battlefield of B and C. In D (which has
"Let" verses only) the invocations are hardly more than a
way of marking off the days—which are frequently dated—
for example:

> Let Reading, house of Reading, rejoice with Synodontites found in
> the fish Synodontes. 27th July N.S. 1762 Lord Jesus have mercy on
> my soul. (D.46)

Many of the names of "houses" seem to be taken from lists
of deaths, marriages, appointments, etc., in almanacs or
or current periodicals, of which Smart evidently had a prompt
and efficient supply.[1] They were jotted down at the rate of
one, or sometimes two, a day. The dates are in the New
Style, contrary to Smart's bias in earlier fragments, and
frequently there are brisk little comments which have an
unmistakable tang of the outside world; for example—

> Let Wing, house of Wing, rejoice with Phlomos a sort of Rush.
> I give the glory to God, thro Christ, for taking the Havannah. Sept^r.
> 30th. 1762.[2]

In spite of the quaint form in which it is cast, there is an
air of normality about all this fragment, and, as the weeks
go on, a wind of suppressed excitement begins to stir. He

[1] See A. Sherbo in *Modern Language Notes*, 1956, pp. 177–82.
[2] Stead notes that the surrender of Havana to Pocock was announced
in the *London Gazette* of 30 September, the very day of this entry.

was now in the seventh year of his "jeopardy," and by all the signs and portents the seventh was to be the last. He was now beginning to receive visitors from the outside world; perhaps this was a result of the lawsuit, *Rex v. Turlington*, 1761, in which a lady had been set free from Turlington's house by a *Habeas Corpus* writ, and Lord Mansfield (a former friend of Smart's, incidentally) had ruled that keepers of these houses had no right to bar a near relative or a physician who wished to visit an inmate.

Samuel Johnson is the only friend whose visit is actually documented; he made a report upon it to Charles Burney, telling him that Smart was tranquil and growing fat, but that he took a fair amount of exercise digging in the garden. He then added—according to Boswell:[1]

> I did not think he ought to be shut up. His infirmities were not noxious to society. He insisted on people praying with him; and I'd as lief pray with Kit Smart as anyone else. Another charge was that he did not love clean linen; and I have no passion for it.

Smart was evidently in a good state when Johnson saw him—except for the dirty linen; but this, certainly a change from earlier habits, may have been due to the economies which asylum-keepers were accustomed to practise in the diet and apparel of their charges.

It was probably this visit Smart was recording about 24 August when he wrote: "Let Johnson, house of Johnson, rejoice with Omphalocarpa a kind of bur. God be gracious to Samuel Johnson." Other visitors recorded in the same way that winter may have been Dr Arne, Michael and Charles Burney, and the Tyers family. An earlier entry of about 12 August may be the first hint of his coming release: "Let Flexney, house of Flexney, rejoice with Triopthalmos—God be gracious to Churchill, Lloyd and especially to Sheels." Flexney was the publisher of all these three men; James Sheeles was a pious clergyman, Charles Churchill an impious

---

[1] Boswell inserts here the story about the alehouse, but, according to Mrs Thrale, that was said on an earlier occasion. There were evidently two occasions when Johnson spoke to Burney about Smart: one (probably in 1760) when he said Smart *should* be shut up, and the other, this one, when he said he should not. Boswell has telescoped them, as he often did with things that were only hearsay to him.

one—but a close friend of the group that were launching the inquiry into private lunatic asylums.

Churchill's earlier career had been ruined, as has been already mentioned, by an unfortunate marriage contracted when he was sixteen, and he had been obliged to take orders for a living. But about 1760 he abandoned his wife and renounced his orders and plunged into politics and literature in London just at the time when John Wilkes was beginning his paper the *North Briton*, against Lord Bute and George III. Churchill's frightful immorality and ferocious powers of invective made him an object of horror to most people but a favourite in the scandalous circles of Sir Francis Dashwood and John Wilkes. Dashwood was the president of the committee of enquiry into private asylums and Wilkes was one of the members. Churchill was already known to Smart, as is testified by the very curious entry in *Jubilate Agno* of December 1759.[1] Churchill (though Smart seems to have known Wilkes also) may have been the link between him and this committee whose hard handling of Turlington coincided so pat with his own release.

At any rate, by 10 November of that year, as another entry shows, he was aware of some negotiations going on in his favour.

The other thing that kept his spirits up during these last months was the liturgical project which he had substituted for *Jubilate Agno*. This was a translation into rhyming verse of the entire psalter (150 psalms, some of them extremely long), coupled with a completely new set of hymns for every feast-day of the Church of England. This formidable labour, besides keeping him busy, served to stop and satisfy in a perfectly normal way that gnawing pseudo-messianic obsession which otherwise could play such evil tricks on him. There are several references to his great work towards the end of *Jubilate Agno*, and one in particular which is no more abnormal than a harmless and pleasant daydream:

The Lord magnify the idea of Smart singing hymns on this day in the eyes of the whole University of Cambridge. Nov[r]. 5th 1762. N.S.

[1] "A papist hath no sentiment God bless CHURCHILL." (B.295.)

Nevertheless I think it has to be admitted that his translation of the psalter did him harm in two ways. Indirectly, because he placed such enormous hopes upon it; he saw it as a stepping-stone to some place of authority in the Church of England from which he could begin to propagate his other reforms for "the revival of Adoration amongst Englishmen." Directly, because so much of the psalter consists of the complaints to God of the persecuted psalmist against his enemies. Although Smart had become perfectly sane in his ordinary dealings with men and things, yet this character of the persecuted prophet had become deeply marked in him. On the other hand, the other notes, which are really more prominent in the psalter, those of sheer adoration, joy and gratitude, became even more deeply engraved; and these in the end were to provide the recurrent spring of hope that saved him. As he wrote in one later, very lovely lyric:

> We never are deserted quite;
> 'Tis by succession of delight
> That love supports his reign.

Meanwhile, as the about-to-be-discarded manuscript of *Jubilate Agno* draws to its close, it is impossible not to share Smart's mounting excitement. On 28 January 1763, not more than a day or two before his release, comes the important entry: "God be gracious to John Sherrat."

Very little can be discovered about this John Sherratt. Yet he was undoubtedly the man who actually opened the door to freedom. For Smart's celebration of his release, published in June or July 1763, was *An Epistle to John Sherratt, Esq.*, which is a curious blend of mysterious allusiveness and plain triumph.

He leaves no doubt that the jeopardy began in 1756:

> Well nigh seven years had fill'd their tale,
> From Winter's urn to Autumn's scale . . .

Or that John Sherratt was the man who actually ended it:

> 'Tis blessing as by God we're told,
> To come and visit friends in hold;
> Which skill is greater in degree
> If goodness set the pris'ner free.

> 'Tis you that have in my behalf
> Produc'd the robe and killed the calf;
> Have hail'd the *restoration day*,
> And bid the loudest music play.

The feat is described as a bold and triumphant naval expedition or cutting-out raid:

> Of such a class in such a sphere
> Shall thy distinguish'd deed appear;
> Whose spirit open and avow'd
> Array'd itself against the crowd,
> With chearfulness so much thine own,
> And all thy motive God alone;
> To run thy keel across the boom,
> And save my vessel from her doom,
> And cut her from the pirate's port,
> Beneath the cannon of the fort,
> With colours fresh and sails unfurl'd,
> Was nobly dar'd to beat the world;
> And stands forever on record
> IF TRUTH AND LIFE BE GOD AND LORD.

The mysteriousness of the poem lies partly in the echoes from Smart's long brooding over the scriptures;[1] partly in the identity of John Sherratt and the means by which he set Smart free. Smart mentions in the poem that Sherratt had been helped by Richard Rolt (Smart's old friend) and by Miss Sheeles, sister of the James Sheeles (lately dead) who had probably visited Smart in August 1762.

The sum of research about John Sherratt is that he was a merchant of St Martin's Lane, Cannon Street; that he had helped Rolt in 1762 in one of Rolt's numerous summonses for debt; that he, or a London merchant of the same name, was appointed British Consul in Carthagena in 1776, where also he came to the aid of a prisoner for debt; that he quarrelled with the Governor there and was himself imprisoned, returning to England after his eventual release.

[1] For example this allusion to the Book of *Wisdom*, xi, 20:
> We reckon all the BOOK of GRACE
> By verses, as the source we trace,
> And in the spirit all is great
> By number, melody and weight.

The *Critical Review* of July 1763 coupled him with Rolt in a slighting reference to Smart's poem. The sketchy picture that emerges is of a pious and possibly eccentric merchant who had an inclination towards helping lame dogs. Smart probably lodged with him and his family for a short period after his release.

As to the means by which he set Smart free, he seems simply to have walked in and "cut him out" under the nose of the keeper. And here it cannot be a mere coincidence that during that very week Mr Turlington and his agent King were facing the House of Commons committee in a state of considerable alarm.

The committee met on 27 January—to inquire into abuses in the reception and retention of persons in private madhouses. Both Dr Monro of Bedlam and Dr Battie of St Luke's were present as expert witnesses. Out of all the hundreds of hard cases at their disposal the committee chose to dwell on three only: one from Miles's house in Hoxton and two from Turlington's house in Chelsea; and all the brunt of the questioning fell upon Turlington and upon his servant, King, who was summoned when Turlington passed everything off on to him. Poor King seems to have been a bit of a simpleton. Asked if he would really shut up a lady on no other evidence than that of another lady who claimed to be her mother, he replied, Oh, most certainly he would. Being asked if he had ever refused anybody whatsoever who was able to pay the board, he answered, No. Dr Battie, the expert, being asked if it were possible for people to be shut up who were not lunatics at all, replied that unfortunately it was not only possible, but that he knew many cases where it had actually happened. Dr Monro, who detested Battie, agreed huffily that no doubt these private places required much stricter supervision.

The lady in question about whom King was questioned had been admitted in September 1762 and then released in October upon a writ of *Habeas Corpus*, granted by Lord Mansfield. Moreover in this case it was not a relative but a mere friend who got permission for a surgeon to demand entrance and examine the lady. In Smart's case no writ or document of any kind has been found about his release; probably the mere threat of one would have been quite sufficient, things being as they were, two days after the House of Commons Inquiry. Turlington certainly could not have afforded to risk another scandal. And even if Smart was not in Turlington's house, he was in some place which did not have a physician to sanction its doings. Without a physician and with all the publicity that was then being given to private madhouses, no keeper would have dared to hold a well-known man like Smart who could still call on a score of influential friends—if he was determined to go.

And Smart was determined to go. He felt he had served, or very nearly, his seven years to win the reward of heavenly wisdom. He had returned from his deep sea voyaging with a great cargo which he was bursting to unload upon the world. The two most engaging things about this moment of his life are: his pent-up enthusiasm about the literary work that lay in front of him, and, secondly, the way in which old friends rallied round to help him after all these years—though they had not the least idea in the world what he was after.

The great work he was about to launch was his translation of the Psalms. It is pretty certain this was completed before his release; it must have been a labour of at least a year, and he was so busy after January 1763, there simply would not have been time for it then. Moreover he immediately set about getting subscribers and trying to find a printer and publisher. Already in the previous December he had learned that Newbery and Carnan were committed to a rival version by a well-known scholar and hymn-writer, James Merrick;[1] but, nothing disturbed, he had written with great generosity and assurance; "Let Merrick, house of Merrick, rejoice. . . . God all-sufficient bless & forward the Psalmist in the Lord Jesus."

The response to Smart's appeal for subscribers was amazing. The list did not appear till a year or two later, owing to

[1] Merrick was the author of the *Benedicite Paraphrased* which, in the recent resurgence of interest in Smart, was confidently but wrongly attributed to him.

delays in printing, but the names began to come in at once. Over seven hundred in number, the nucleus of them is a roll-call of all who had found cause to love him in the past. His family: Marianne of *The Hop Garden* and her Irish husband (ten copies), Margaret and her husband, Dr Hunter; his aristocratic patrons: the Earl of Darlington and several Vanes and Delavals and about twenty more of the nobility; John Wilkes and Charles Churchill who had probably helped towards his release. Then a great concourse of old London friends: Arthur Murphy, Garrick, Hogarth, the Tyers family, Charles Burney, Dr Arne, and several writers not yet mentioned in this book, William Cowper (himself but lately recovered from derangement), Thomas and Joseph Warton, Smollett, Akenside, Cumberland and Woty. Especially pleasing is the name of the old rapscallion William Kenrick, to whom Smart devoted a poem (*Reason and Imagination*, to be mentioned later) in gratitude for the reconciliation. Others who are known only by the poems Smart addressed to them: John Sherratt, the Sheeles family, "Rev. Mr. Tyler," "Rev. Mr Morgan Powell," and a splendid soldier, evidently a great hero of Smart's, Brigadier-General Sir William Draper,[1] who ordered no less than forty copies.

But perhaps the most heartening of all for Smart was the great rally of Cambridge men, especially the Fellows of Pembroke: Randall, Boyce, Stonhewer, Anguish, Gordon, Jermyn Pratt, Addison—not to omit Thomas Gray and Mason.

Mr Brittain comments: "Conspicuous by their absence are Mrs Smart, the Newbery-Carnan family, and Dr Johnson." This, as usual with Mr Brittain, is a little hard on Anna-Maria: one would not expect a man's wife to be listed among his subscribers. Newbery and Carnan seem to have helped Smart financially in other ways this year, but they were already committed to a rival publication when Smart launched his. The absence of Johnson, however, is harder

---

[1] Cf. *Jubilate Agno*: "For I bless God that I am of the same seed as Ehud, Mutius Scaevola, and Colonel Draper." Draper is less happily known as one of the victims of *Junius's* pen.

to explain, for there is no evidence of any break in the friendship; on the contrary, on 24 May 1763, Boswell on his first meeting with Johnson records this speech:

Madness frequently discovers itself merely by unnecessary deviation from the usual modes of the world. My poor friend Smart shewed the disturbance of his mind by falling upon his knees and saying his prayers in the street or in any other unusual place. Now although, rationally speaking, it is a greater madness not to pray at all than to pray as Smart did, I am afraid there are so many who do not pray that their understanding is not called in question.

Although Johnson in his Boswellian cloak seems rather ponderous and distant here, he was still glad to be known as Smart's friend. His remark to Burney, inserted in the same place by Boswell,[1] is warmer and more human: "I'd as lief pray with Kit Smart as anyone else." But one cannot be certain whether this was spoken before or after 1763. It may be, as Tom Tyers hints in his reminiscences of Johnson,[2] that the friendship was not maintained in later years. But one distinctly unfriendly remark recorded by Boswell much later should probably be struck out of the canon. Asked for comment on Smart and Derrick, Johnson is supposed to have replied: "There is no settling the point of precedency between a louse and a flea." But in the original story, which was told by Morgann as another example of Johnson's spirit of contradiction, there is no mention at all of Smart; the comparison was between *Boyce* and Derrick.[3]

On the other hand, it is quite certain that Smart immediately after his release set up a barrier against his family, and therefore perhaps against anyone who sympathized with his family. There was a story current in these first months that he intended to "prosecute the people who had confined him," and biographers have supposed that this referred to Newbery and Carnan. But I think that the "adversaries" to whom Smart attributed his second confinement—he prays against them in *Jubilate Agno* in August 1759 and again in November 1762—are more likely to have been his cousin

[1] Quoted above, p. 129.
[2] G. Birkbeck Hill, *Johnsonian Miscellanies*, ii. 364.
[3] See Forster's *Oliver Goldsmith* (ed. 1877, I, 342), citing the *European Magazine*, September 1796 (xxx, 160).

Francis Smart (who finally mortgaged Snotterton in 1763) and Richard Smart, the London solicitor, who seems to have had Christopher excluded from inheriting. There is no record, however, of any Smart lawsuit at this time.

The rumour of the lawsuit and the news about Smart during the first months after his release come as on two former occasions in his life (1746 and 1759) from the correspondence of Thomas Gray. Or rather, in this case it is his friend Mason, to whom Gray replies. Mason, a good-hearted busy-body, wrote from London in June 1763:

> I have got about 10 subscribers to Smart & dont know how to transmit him the money. Stonhewer advises me to keep it, as he hears he is in somebody's hands who may cheat him. I have seen his Song to David & from thence conclude him as mad as ever. But this I mention only that one should endeavour to assist him as effectually as possible which one cannot do without the mediation of a third person. If you know any body now in London (for Stonhewer has left it) whom I can write to on this subject pray tell me. Tis said in the papers he is prosecuting the people who confined him. If so, assisting him at present is only throwing ones money to the lawyers.

Gray replied in July:

> I think it may be time enough to send poor Smart the money you have been so kind to collect for him, when he has dropped his lawsuit. which I dont doubt must go against him if he pursues it. Gordon (who lives here) knows and interests himself about him: from him I shall probably know if he can be persuaded to drop his design. There is a Mr Anguish in Town (with whom, I fancy, you were once acquainted) he probably can best inform you of his condition & motions, for I hear he continues to be very friendly to him.

Thus, from Mason's humdrum world of duty and dullness, so alien to the glowing garden of Smart's mind, we learn of the great event of his life. There is the growing number of subscribers to his *Translation of the Psalms of David*. Then, with a sickening thud, or at least with a sodden sense of anti-climax, the biographer realizes that the great moment in Smart's life—the moment to which all his efforts and sufferings and exaltations must inevitably seem tensed and pre-destined—has been allowed to slip out miserably in Mason's sentence: "I have seen his Song to David & from thence conclude him as mad as ever."

ELEVEN

❖

The Immortal Song

ON 8 April M. Fletcher of the Oxford Theatre in St
Paul's Churchyard issued *A Song to David* by Christopher Smart, M.A. (price one shilling), every copy signed by
the author. At the end of the poem were advertised proposals for printing by subscription *A New Translation
of the Psalms of David*, to which would be added *A Set
of Hymns for the Fasts and Festivals of the Church of England*. What suggests itself irresistibly is that from the great
mass of his psalm-translations there leaped this quintessential distillation of them, the immortal *Song to David*;
his step forth into liberty coinciding with a sudden coordination of brain and hand and mental vision; it was "the
fine delight that fathers thought" which, as a later religious
poet describes it:

> Breathes once and, quenched faster than it came,
> Leaves yet the mind a mother of immortal song . . .
> The widow of an insight lost she lives, with aim
> Now known and hand at work now never wrong.

It is extremely difficult to think of Smart's translation (or
paraphrase it is, rather) of the psalms except as a background to the *Song to David*. The sheer bulk of the translation, well over fifty thousand words (for Smart, besides
being verbose, gives several alternative renderings), defies
detailed criticism in a book like this. Moreover, the modern
reader, unused to the rhymed versions which were bound up

with every eighteenth-century prayer-book, will be repelled by a certain hurdy-gurdy element—especially in passages that have become hallowed in the Vulgate or the Authorized Version.

Although he hoped for much greater things from his paraphrase, probably its main interest lies in its being an unintentional rehearsal for the *Song to David*. Not that the *Song* is a patchwork from bits of the psalms but rather that, when Smart in a clear light laid down the bold, strong lines of his plan, there was a positive rush of phrases, images and actual rhymes from the psalm-translation to fill in certain places. But only certain places: there is much in the *Song* which comes from other parts of the Bible, and much from Smart's own theology and philosophy—as *Jubilate Agno* bears frequent witness. Above all, there was that gift of "impression" which stamped his mental vision on the words and phrases as they came tumbling out.

The main lines of his plan have been reduced by Professor Havens to multiples of 3 and 7, and there is no doubt that sacred numbers played a large part in Smart's conception. But I think Browning's first impression of the plan still remains the most enlightening; he saw it in the proportions of a great cathedral, with the purpose and embellishments of a cathedral, and he heard in it the swelling or piercing rise and fall of the organ music that fills a great cathedral.

It opens with three rather stiff stanzas of invocation—three steps, Browning called them; then suddenly you are in a nave or arcade of twelve statues. These are the twelve virtues that make up the perfect man, modelled on the twelve prophetic blessings of Jacob. They had been the subject of much confused meditation in *Jubilate Agno*; but here their sudden introduction is very crisp and efficient:

> Great, valiant, pious, good, and clean,
> Sublime, contemplative, serene,
> Strong, constant, pleasant, wise!
> Bright effluence of exceeding grace;
> Best man!—the swiftness and the race,
> The peril, and the prize!

There is a stanza for each virtue, for example:

> Pleasant—and various as the year;
> Man, soul, and angel, without peer,
>   Priest, champion, sage and boy;
> In armour, or in ephod clad,
> His pomp, his piety was glad;
>   Majestic was his joy.

Then a dark and tender connecting verse, like an archway—

> His muse, bright angel of his verse,
> Gives balm for all the thorns that pierce,
>   For all the pangs that rage;
> Blest light, still gaining on the gloom,
> The more than Michal of his bloom,
>   The Abishag of his age.

—leads into what Browning called a radiant chapel "of nine
leaded windows, of rich colour and fantastic design, representing the subject of David's poetry . . . four on each side
of the church and a rose over the entrance." It may be only
a coincidence—Browning certainly was not aware of it—but
one of the most distinctive features of Durham Cathedral,
which Smart knew so well, is the Chapel of the Nine Windows
with a great rose window over the centre. The themes of
David's verse were the Holy Spirit and all his works, visible
and invisible. Here is a typical stanza:

> The world—the clustring spheres he made,
> The glorious light, the soothing shade,
>   Dale, champaign, grove, and hill;
> The multitudinous abyss,
> Where secrecy remains in bliss,
>   And wisdom hides her skill.

There follow three intermediary stanzas and then, in the
place where the choir would be (Browning again), "we see
seven pillars, finely carved, which symbolize the wisdom of
God as it appears in the seven days of creation."

> The pillars of the Lord are seven,
> Which stand from earth to topmost heav'n;
>   His wisdom drew the plan;
> His WORD accomplished the design
> From brightest gem to deepest mine,
>   From CHRIST enthron'd to man.

The reference to the seven pillars is to *Proverbs* xi, 1. Each of the seven stanzas that follow is introduced by a Greek letter, Α, Γ, Η, Θ, Ι, Σ, Ω. In spite of this cryptogram appearance I think that the stanzas illustrate the depth of Smart's christian orthodoxy and are therefore worth going into. The suggestion that the letters are Masonic symbols should be set aside. There is no evidence for it; rather the reverse. A writer in *Miscellanea Latomorum* (October 1924) states: "I am unable to offer any suggestion as to the reason for selecting these particular letters of the Greek alphabet." The Curator of the Grand Lodge Library, London, through whose courtesy I was shown this article, adds: "I, too, am defeated in spite of my familiarity with the ritual of numerous masonic degrees."

The meaning of the letters will appear, if it appears at all, from an elucidation of the stanzas. Clues to the elucidation are supplied in abundance, sometimes in the rest of the poem, more frequently in *Jubilate Agno*, occasionally in the author's translation of the psalms and his hymns. The first clue, from *Jubilate Agno* (C.18–33)—

> For Christ being *A* and *Ω* is all the intermediate letters without doubt.
>
> For there is a mystery in numbers.

—indicates that the letters should be taken as the numbers for which they stood in classical Greek. But its more important meaning is that the seven stanzas describe seven aspects or appearances of Christ, the Word made Flesh. This is strongly confirmed by the last line of the introductory stanza—

> From CHRIST enthron'd to man.

The plan of the seven pillars reaches from Christ enthroned in glory to Christ the poor man on earth. This has to be taken along with the plain meaning that the pillars stand for the successive "days" of creation. Each "day" therefore (and each stanza) will represent not only a stage in creation but an aspect of the mystery of God becoming Man. This means that the incarnation of God the Son and the creation of the universe are part of the same plan.

We are helped here by two tenets of the great Cambridge and Jacobite divine, William Law, whose theology Smart seems to have shared. Law held, in common with some Catholic theologians, that Christ was literally "the first-born of creation"; that he was first manifested to the angels in some created form; that the "war in heaven" was a consequence; and that after the fall of the rebel angels he was "hidden" in human nature till the moment of his conception in the womb of the Virgin Mary:

> From that time [i.e. after the sin of Lucifer] the incarnation of the Son of God began, because he was from that time entered again into human nature, as the seed or beginning of its Salvation, hidden under the veil of the Law, and not made manifest till he was born in the holy and highly blessed Virgin Mary.

In his translation of the Psalms, Smart makes some additions to the text which show that he held the same view about earlier theophanies or manifestations of Christ. In Psalm 16 he speaks of "the fiends that fell Thy holy one to stay"; and in Psalm 68 he says of Jesus Christ:

> In other days before the sev'n
> Upon that ante-mundane heav'n
> In glorious pomp he rode.

Of the six days of creation, Law held that the first three represent the creation of the paradisal order whose harmony was spoilt by sin; the second three represent the restoration of that harmony in a lower form—"so that the outward condition and frame of visible nature is a plain manifestation of that spiritual world from which it is descended." The seventh day, *Omega*, is the consummation of the restoration and comes back full circle to *Alpha*. This is implicit in the text of *Revelation*: "I am Alpha, I am Omega . . . the beginning and the end."

To take the stanzas in their order:

> Alpha, the cause of causes, first
> In station, fountain whence the burst
>   Of light, and blaze of day;
> Whence bold attempt, and brave advance,
> Have motion, life and ordinance,
>   And heaven itself its stay.

Alpha is the original created light of the word, "Let there be light." It is also the reflection of the Son coming forth from the Father, "*Deum de Deo, Lumen de Lumine.*" This original light, both spiritual and physical, is "the light that enlighteneth every man that cometh into this world," spoken of by St John in his first chapter whence most of Smart's thought in this stanza is derived. The opening of St John's gospel has always been taken by Christians as complementing the opening of the book of Genesis.

The next stanza, the *Gamma* stanza, is more intricate:

> Gamma supports the glorious arch
> On which angelic legions march,
>   And is with sapphires pav'd;
> Thence the fleet clouds are sent adrift
> And thence the painted folds, that lift
>   The crimson veil, are wav'd.

Gamma stands for the creation of the upper heaven and of the angels who are its denizens. The images in lines 5, 1 and 2— the painted folds, the glorious arch and the marching angels— are borrowed by Smart from his own translation of three verses in Psalm 104: ". . . who stretchest out the heavens like a curtain . . . who maketh the clouds his chariot . . . who maketh his angels spirits, his ministers a flaming fire." In Smart's translation he takes three stanzas for the three verses; in the first a waving curtain hangs in folds from heaven's dome; in the second it waves aside to reveal the glorious arch; in the third the flame-like angels move between heaven and earth. In the *Gamma* stanza all these three images coalesce. The evocation becomes more distinct in line 3, "And is with sapphires pav'd." This comes from *Exodus* xxiv, 10:

> And they saw the God of Israel: and there was under his feet as it were a paved work of sapphire stone, and as it were the body of heaven in his clearness.

This vision introduces the theme which occupies the rest of *Exodus*, namely, the Ark of the Covenant, the institution of priests to serve it, the angels who protect it, and the "painted folds" of the veil of the tabernacle.

Line 4: "Thence the fleet clouds are sent adrift," beautifully completes the picture by stating the office of the angels, which is to carry prayers from the earthly altar to the heavenly altar, in the context of *Revelation* viii, 3–5:

> And another angel came and stood at the altar having a golden censer . . . and the smoke of the incense which came with the prayers of the saints, ascended up before God out of the angel's hand.

The "crimson veil" is used again by Smart in his hymn on *The Presentation of Christ in the Temple*, and there it connotes the communion service. The total picture, thus, is of Christ the "Angel" and High-Priest of creation, whose ministers are priests on earth and angels in heaven. It is a very ancient picture in Christian liturgy and occurs in the Roman Mass, in a prayer after the consecration where the priest begs:

> that these things may be carried up by the hands of thy holy Angel on to thy altar on high beneath the eyes of thy divine majesty; that we who communicate at this altar below the most holy Body and Blood of thy Son may be filled with all grace and heavenly blessing.[1]

Gamma, the number three, denotes spiritual perfection; so it is used here of Christ, the Holy One, apex and spear-point of creation.

The third stanza is *Eta*. The work of the third day was the creation of all growing things: plants, trees, flowers. But here it is taken for the planting of the earthly paradise. Its symbol is something which could be either a tree or a pillar:

> Eta with living sculpture breathes,
> With verdant carvings, flow'ry wreathes
> Of never-wasting bloom,
> In strong relief his goodly base
> All instruments of labour grace,
> The trowel, spade, and loom.

Eta is seven. Seven, three upon four, signifies perfect growth: three for perfection of soul, four for bodily perfection, and seven is the union of both. In mediaeval art it is generally depicted as a triangle on a square or a conical turret on four

---

[1] This is the thought in one of the very last poems he wrote:
> Thus in the height it shall be done
> And thus the penitent be blest.

see p. 190.

walls. Smart's symbol, however, which could be either the tree of paradise or the pillar of wisdom, is perfectly suited to his purpose. The immortal flowers and branches of spiritual perfection in the first half of the stanza, and the "goodly base" of bodily perfection in the second, both could belong to a tree or to a column. One thinks of the passage in the sixteenth century *Rites of Durham* describing the old Cathedral:

> From pillar to pillar was set up a border very artificially wrought in stone with marvellous fine colours, very curiously and excellently finely gilt with branches and flowers, the more that a man did look at it the more desires he had, and the greater his affection to behold it.

The picture of Christ which unifies the stanza is that created form, whatever it was, which the Son of God took when he walked with Adam "in the garden in the cool of the day" (*Genesis*, iii, 8). You could call it "the Paradisal Christ," or "Christ in Nature"—or even, remembering Piero della Francesca, "Christ the Gardener."

The fourth stanza, *Theta*, commemorates creation of sun and moon, the lights of earth and lower heaven. *Theta* is eight, which stands for marriage—four upon four, the union of two bodily perfections.

> Next Theta stands to the Supreme—
> Who formed in number, sign and scheme,
>   Th' illustrious lights that are;
> And one address'd his saffron robe,
> And one, clad in a silver globe,
>   Held rule with ev'ry star.

The connection of sun and moon with marriage might seem an arbitrary one, if it were not something on which Smart held very definite ideas:

> For the Sun's at work to make me a garment & the Moon is at work for my wife . . .
> For the WEDDING GARMENTS of all men are prepared in the SUN against the day of acceptation.
> For the Wedding Garments of all women are prepared in the MOON against the day of their purification . . .
> For the SUN is an intelligence and an angel of the human form.
> For the MOON is an intelligence and an angel in shape like a woman.
> For they are together in the spirit every night like man and wife.

What was going on inside Smart's mind when he wrote these lines in *Jubilate Agno* is not at all clear, but their compressed and objective meaning has quite clearly been transferred to *Theta*. The stanza coalesces to form that picture of the Messiah which is present throughout the psalms and canticles and prophets: Christ the Bridegroom. The Bride is Israel, the chosen people of the Old Testament, whose mission is handed over in the New Testament to the universal church and the whole human race. The relation of marriage to the "great mystery" of Christ and his church is stated by St Paul in the fifth chapter to the Ephesians (22–33).

The fifth stanza, *Iota*, for the day assigned to the production of birds and fishes, runs:

> Iota's tuned to choral hymns
> Of those that fly, while he that swims
> In thankful safety lurks;
> And foot, and chapitre, and niche
> The various histories enrich
> Of God's recorded works.

In the other stanzas the meaning of the letter or number appears from the content of the stanza: three for Angel, seven for perfect growth, eight for marriage. But with *iota* (nine) it is different; we are told in the first line what the number signifies, and are left to puzzle out what aspect of the incarnation is contained in the rest of the stanza. Smart, in the passage of *Jubilate Agno* about the letters or numbers between alpha and omega (C.18–33), says "For Nine is a very good number and harmonious"; this jumps at once with the first lines "Iota's tuned to choral hymns Of those that fly."[1] The sequence in Smart's mind: Iota—nine—harmony—choirs of angels—birds—is clear from *Jubilate Agno* (B.122):

Let Cherub rejoice with Cherub who is a bird and a blessed Angel. For I bless God for every feather from the wren in the sedge to the CHERUBS & their MATES.

[1] It also shows Smart is following the simple use of letters for numbers α–ω=1–24, as in the numeration of the books of Homer, not the later form in which the alphabet, expanded by three letters, was used for digits, tens and hundreds.

But what about the fish? Well, still trying to follow Smart's mind, we find this passage—from B.122 onwards—continuing with a list of the apostles and ancestors and intimate friends of Jesus Christ each accompanied by a fish. Between the apostles and ancestors comes his Mother:

> Let Mary rejoice with the Maid—blessed be the name of the immaculate CONCEPTION.

By "immaculate conception" is meant here the conceiving of Jesus by Mary while remaining a virgin. "Maid" is also a name for the fish *Raia batis* and *Raia clavata*. There is the same sort of play on words as in the virga-virgo antiphon of Our Lady:

> Virga Jesse floruit. Virgo Deum et hominem genuit, pacem
> Deus reddidit, in se reconcilians ima summis.

And there is the same idea, I think, of the reconciliation of heights with depths, suggested by the coupling of birds with fish. *Iota*, then (nine being maidenhood as well as harmony), would stand for the descent of Christ into the womb of the Virgin, announced by the archangel Gabriel.

Sigma, the next stanza—the creation of man among the beasts—celebrates the nativity of Christ, his manifestation as true man. This is clear from the last line of the stanza: "For ocular belief":

> Sigma presents the social droves
> With him that solitary roves
>   And man of all the chief;
> Fair on whose face, and stately frame,
> Did God impress his hallow'd name
>   For ocular belief.

All the stanza except the last line could apply to the First Adam who bore the image and likeness of his Creator. But the last line can only apply to Christ, the Second Adam; for he alone of mankind by his actual appearance compelled belief in God. This is often stated in St John's gospel and first epistle; and it is echoed by Smart in a stanza which comes shortly after those of the seven pillars:

> There is but One who ne'er rebell'd,
> But One by passion unimpell'd,
> By pleasures unintice't;
> He from himself his semblance sent,
> Grand object of his own content,
> And saw the God in CHRIST.

Sigma, therefore, signifies Christ the true man, poor and suffering, either in his actual nativity when his birth among the beasts of the stall was a sign to the shepherds, or perhaps at his baptism when the voice from heaven proclaimed his divinity and he then went into the wilderness "and was with the beasts."

Unfortunately as a number (*Sigma* is eighteen) it appears to have no significance whatsoever; and this makes a bad break.[1] But the sequence is restored by *Omega*, which not only signifies consummation in general, but for Smart in particular it signified twenty-four, the number for consummation.

> For the Four and Twenty Elders of the Revelation are Four and Twenty Eternities. For their Four and Twenty Crowns are their respective Consummations.

Omega is the sign for what the Greek Fathers called the "apokatasasis," the restoration of all things.

> OMEGA! GREATEST and the BEST
> Stands sacred to the day of rest,
> For gratitude and thought;
> Which blessed the world upon his pole,
> And gave the universe his goal,
> And clos'd th' infernal draught.

Omega is the day of rest not only for the Creator but for the Redeemer. On Holy Saturday Christ "descended into hell" and "closed the infernal draught," i.e. the down-sucking wind from the abyss. He conquered sin and destroyed death. Thence follows the inevitable roll of triumph: "He rose again from the dead, he ascended into heaven, sitteth at the right hand of God the Father Almighty." Thus *Omega* returns to *Alpha* in a circle. The sequence "From Christ enthroned to man" goes back to Christ enthroned, but this

[1] As a letter, however, Smart says that *S* stands for Soul or Salvation.

time bearing with him human nature made immortal. *Omega* is Christ the "Pantokrator" of Greek theology.

There are several points in which Smart's doctrines seem to stem from Greek theology.[1] But it is impossible to add more to a chapter already overladen with theology. Moreover there still remains the second and more beautiful half of the *Song to David*.

After the passage of the seven pillars there comes an "exercise on the decalogue" which ends with the conclusion that joyful praise is the best service we can offer God; and then come twenty-one stanzas, the famous "ADORATION" stanzas, which to many people form the most attractive part of the poem. The word ADORATION is swung up and down, from line to line of each stanza, through the four seasons and the five senses, giving an extraordinary impression of richness; here, for example, are the three on Spring:

> Rich almonds colour to the prime
> For ADORATION; tendrils climb,
>   And fruit-trees pledge their gems;
> And Ivis, with her gorgeous vest,
> Builds for her eggs her cunning nest,
>   And bell-flowers bow their stems.
>
> With vinous syrup cedars sprout;
> From rocks pure honey gushing out,
>   For ADORATION springs;
> All scenes of painting croud the map
> Of nature; to the mermaid's pap[2]
>   The scaled infant clings.
>
> The spotted ounce and playsome cubs
> Run rustling 'mongst the flow'ring shrubs,
>   And lizards feed the moss;
> For ADORATION beasts embark,
> While waves upholding halcyon's ark
>   No longer roar and toss.

[1] These points, for example, in St Gregory of Nyssa: (1) "apokatastasis" already mentioned; (2) the "passionlessness" ("apathia") of God; (3) the "eikon" (the perfect image) being the stone in the ring on Christ's finger; (4) the murder and hatred in the psalms changed to moral qualities of self-conquest.

[2] The mermaid, which has shocked some critics as a non-Christian intrusion, is actually a feature of the stonework of Durham Cathedral.

The conclusion, pressed down and running over, consists of fifteen stanzas: five groups of three, "five statues," says Browning, "on the pinnacle that crowns the church." But once again Durham Cathedral is more accurate than Browning's imaginary cathedral. On the great stone screen (the Neville Screen) between the present altar and the old shrine, there are five towering pinnacles, each with three tiers of niches for statues. In each triad of the poem some quality is lifted up from earth to the human soul and thence to Christ (or to David typifying Christ). Here is the triad on "Beauty," perhaps the loveliest stanzas in the whole poem. They show also how Smart had quite erased the slight taint of "Catharism" discernible in *Jubilate Agno*:

> Beauteous the fleet before the gale;
> Beauteous the multitudes in mail,
>   Ranked arms and crested heads:
> Beauteous the garden's umbrage mild,
> Walk, water, meditated wild,
>   And all the bloomy beds.
>
> Beauteous the moon full on the lawn;
> And beauteous, when the veil's withdrawn,
>   The virgin to her spouse:
> Beauteous the temple, deck'd and fill'd,
> When to the heav'n of heav'ns they build
>   Their heart-directed vows.
>
> Beauteous, yea beauteous more than these,
> The shepherd king upon his knees,
>   For his momentous trust;
> With wish of infinite conceit,
> For man, beast, mute, the small and great,
>   And prostrate dust to dust.

The poem ends with a swelling crash, and a falling trumpet-peal of "glory":

> Glorious the sun in mid career;
> Glorious th' assembled fires appear;
>   Glorious the comet's train:
> Glorious the trumpet and alarm,
> Glorious th' almighty stretched-out arm;
>   Glorious th' enraptured main.

Glorious the northern lights a-stream;
Glorious the song, when God's the theme;
Glorious the thunder's roar:
  Glorious hosannah from the den;
Glorious the catholic amen;
  Glorious the martyr's gore.

Glorious,—more glorious, is the crown
Of Him that brought salvation down,
  By meekness, called thy Son;
Thou at stupendous truth believ'd
And now the matchless deed's atchiev'd,
DETERMINED, DARED, and DONE.

There is a noble audacity about the *Song* that carries listeners triumphantly over its occasional weaknesses. Only genius could make pure goodness as piercingly attractive as Smart has done. One could go on indefinitely trying to analyse the flash-points of his genius—the interplay of concrete and abstract, natural and artefact, exotic and familiar—and so on. But, to me, it is more relevant to point out that all the best and sanest in Smart went to the making of this poem: his "Franciscan" love of God and of God's creatures; his scholarship and his meditative reading; his happy childhood and boyhood; his happy (while it lasted) marriage and parenthood, and the acutely sensitive and objective images which he retained of these happy experiences. If he never again wrote anything so good, it is probably because he was never again so truly and selflessly happy.

I can see no evidence that his happiness was a result of obsessive madness, or that he could not have written this poem if he had not been mad. Rather the other way round. If it had not been for his obsession, there is no evident reason why he should not have produced other great poems on a par with *A Song to David*. Unfortunately, no sooner was it produced than he threw away his "Franciscan" gladness and began to assume the unnatural, wry-necked posture of the misunderstood prophet.

TWELVE

Strains and Quarrels

SMART was now living in pleasant lodgings in his old bachelor haunts of St. James's Park; his house, kept by very decent people, had a terrace overlooking the park and a door leading into it. Here he devoted himself to writing and the business of writing, but not grudging time to receive and visit friends. The dull reaction to *A Song to David* he regarded as only a temporary setback; he was planning to publish it again in a more favourable atmosphere as an appendix to his psalms and hymns. It had come out in April when all the town was in an uproar over Wilkes's "No. 45" of the *North Briton* and the "General Warrant" for arrests which followed it.

The *Monthly* and *Critical* Reviews had spared time for the *Song* in a manner really more hesitant than hostile, which under the circumstances is hardly to be wondered at. The Whig *Monthly* produced the famous story (quoted in Chapter One) about its being scratched on the madhouse wall, and kept harping on Smart's supposed infirmity:

> From the sufferings of this ingenious gentleman, we could not but expect the performance before us to be greatly irregular, but we shall certainly characterize it more justly, if we call it irregularly great.

But they also spoke of its "grandeur" and "majesty of thought."

The Tory *Critical*, deprived of its founder-editor, Smollett, and anxious to avoid unpopularity, spared Smart's sanity, but made vague insinuations against his supposedly Popish doctrine:

Without venturing to criticize on the propriety of a Protestant's offering up either hymns or prayers to the dead, we must be of opinion that great rapture and devotion is discernable in this ecstatic song. It is a fine piece of ruins.

In the rapid stream of fashion Smart was already considered a back-number, but his reputation was still too great, his friendships too influential, for him to be treated with anything but cautious respect. The literary *parvenu*, Boswell, who had just picked up his name from Johnson's conversation, wrote to Dalrymple (30 July 1763) with his odd mixture of quick insight and complacency:

> I have sent you Smart's *Song to David*, which is a very curious composition, being a strange mixture of *dun obscure* and glowing genius at times. I have also sent some poems which he has lately published. His Genius and Imagination is very pretty. The other pieces have shivers of genius here and there, but are often ludicrously low. Poor man, he has been relieved from his confinement, but not from his unhappy disorder. However, he has it not at any great height. He is not a poet of the first rank.

"Shivers of genius" is good, and "ludicrously low" is unfortunately true enough in some cases, as will be seen. The new poems mentioned by Boswell had appeared that very month.

Smart was determined to get back into the contemporary stream. His July volume of poems, entitled *Reason and Imagination*, contained the fable of that name dedicated to his old enemy and new friend, Kenrick; the "Epistle to John Sherrat" and two patriotico-religious odes, one to General Draper, the other to Admiral Pocock beginning with this remarkable verse:

> When Christ, the seaman, was aboard,
>   Swift as an arrow to the *White*,
> While Ocean his rude rapture roar'd,
>   The vessel gain'd the Haven with delight.
> We therefore first to him the song renew,
>   Then sing of Pocock's praise, and make
>   the point in view.

In the title piece, "Reason and Imagination," we share to some extent Smart's own view of his spiritual status. He is evidently resolved to be "*in* the world, yet not *of* it." Reason is depicted as a philosopher studying the Book of Wisdom in a lonely hermitage.

> Before, a river deep and still;
> Behind, a rocky soaring hill.

Imagination is a beautiful lady, painted with all Smart's sensuous power, who warns the hermit that without her he will come to grief:

> The Doctors soon will find a flaw,
> And lock you up in chains and straw.

But if he will submit to her, she promises:

> I'll bring you to the early cars,
> By dragons drawn above the stars;
> To colours of Arabian glow;
> And to the heart-dilating show
> Of paintings, which surmount the life:
> At once your tut'ress and your wife.

To Smart, in his state of heightened sensibility bruised by the world's indifference, the temptation to slip into an intoxicated dream-world must have been a powerful one. It says much—I think—for the new strength and balance of his character that he was content to compromise; he needed his imagination for the work before him, but as an ally, not a mistress; a means, not an end:

> 'Soft, soft,' (says Reason) 'lovely friend;
> Tho' to a parley I attend,
> I cannot take thee for a mate;
> I'm lost, if e'er I change my state.
> But whensoe'er your raptures rise,
> I'll try to come with my supplies;
> To muster up my sober aid,
> What time your lively pow'rs invade;
> To act conjointly in the war
> On dullness, whom we both abhor.'

Smart, however, used the back pages of *Reason and Imagination* to make a very angry reply, in which neither reason nor imagination was very happily employed, to the *Critical Review*'s aspersions on his Protestant orthodoxy:

The first Part of this insidious Cavil is a stupendous impudence against the Truth of CHRIST JESUS, who has most confidently

154

affirmed this same DAVID to be alive in his Argument for the Resurrection. . . . It is a pity that Men should be permitted to set up for Critics, who make it so evident that they have neither RELIGION nor LEARNING; since *candour* cannot subsist without the former, and there can be no Authority to pronounce *Judgment* without the latter.

One can sympathize with Smart's anger, but it was unreasonable of him to look for theology in a London periodical. The *Critical*, in its brief review of *Reason and Imagination*, passed his comments off with a shrug. The *Monthly* renewed its insinuations against Smart's sanity, but this time in a more wounding manner:

> Instead of entering on the merit of these poems, we shall transcribe a few lines from Milton's SAMSON, and leave our Readers to make the application:
>
>> This, this is he; softly awhile,
>> Let us not break in upon him;
>> O change beyond report, thought, or belief!

Smart's reply was to publish another slim volume of verse in November 1763 (with the title *Munificence and Modesty*) and reserve its back pages for another violent personal attack, this time on the *Monthly Review*. The *Critical* had been attacked on behalf of David and doctrine, but it was in defence of Smart's own reputation that the *Monthly* was "summoned to the Bar of the Publick to answer the following questions":

> Whether there is any Thing they hate so much as Truth and Merit?
> Whether they have not depended upon their malignity, for the sale of their Book from the beginning?
> Whether the writings of Mr Smart in particular (his Prize Poems excepted) have not been constantly misrepresented to the Publick by their despicable Pamphlet?
> Whether the Reverend Mr Langhorne has not the poetical department of the Monthly Review?
> Whether a certain scandalous fellow, who has oppressed Mr Smart for these many years, did not wait upon Griffiths, and complain that he had been treated too mildly in a former Review?
> Whether the said scandalous fellow did not give Griffiths and others Money to defame Mr Smart, as far as they dared?
> Whether, if this was the case, they do not act their Mischief without motive, and serve the Devil from affection?

Smart was raking up grievances which went right back to the days when Hill of *The Hilliad* was writing for Griffiths' *Monthly*. It may seem strange that a man who has just spent years in ascetic seclusion wrestling with his soul should have retained so much of his old vanity and quarrelsomeness and lost only, alas, his old gaiety and sense of humour. But in fact it is not to be wondered at. Smart had broken off his period of seclusion, leaving his main problem—the nature of his mission, and the sense of his own importance that went with it—unexplored and unsettled. The unfinished neophyte, scorning worldly wisdom yet refusing (as Smart, to his credit, was refusing) to fall back on histrionic fanaticism, is at a disadvantage in dispute with his thicker-skinned mundane counterpart; he is much more liable to surface explosions of vanity and even of hysteria, since his main energies and controls are in tension towards a different and (to him) much more important objective. Smart was all keyed up for the publication of his psalms and hymns which (he felt) was the first great step towards the still obscure goal ahead of him.

Had he mingled a little worldly wisdom with his prized "heavenly wisdom," he would have extended his forgiveness of Kenrick to the reviewers of the *Monthly* and *Critical* as well; for to make them hostile, and then to *mind* their hostility, was to invite the worst of both worlds. And wisdom, too, whether worldly or heavenly, would have bade him pay attention to this sentence of the *Monthly*'s reply in its not uncomplimentary review of *Munificence and Modesty*:

> As it appears to him so unpardonably criminal to affix any limitation whatever to the praises which he thinks due to all his Writings, he may rest assured that he will, for the future, have very little cause to be offended with us, on that account.

It might be urged that attempts to judge Smart's behaviour at this distance of time are useless and unfair, since the man was, as expressly stated by his critics, not in full possession of his faculties. But the very malice of these insinuations impugns their truth. I think the evidence will show that Smart, though living under a strain, was fully responsible for his actions, right up till nearly the end of his life.

In one way, at least, he was taking steps to ward off unnecessary unpopularity. He had become aware that his doctrines laid him open to suspicions of "popery," and he was beginning to make efforts to dispel such suspicions. An example of this was the title-piece, "Munificence and Modesty"; the inspiration for it came from "a painting by Guido"—obviously "The Coronation of the Virgin" by Guido Reni, in which Mary is depicted as a peasant girl being crowned by a multitude of angels.[1] But in the poem there is no mention of Mary, and all is treated as a fable.

Similarly, in the poem to John Sherratt, Smart had written:

> To build the great foundation laid
> By one sublime, transcendent maid.

Clearly in the context the reference is to the Church of Christ and the Mother of Christ. But Smart added a hasty footnote that "the one sublime transcendent maid" was "Miss A.F.S. of Queens Square."

Almost every quarter was now seeing some new production from Smart. In April 1764 came an oratorio entitled *Hannah*, for which the music had been written by the same Worgan who had done his *Solemn Dirge* twelve years before. Strange echoes for Smart! But the piece, performed in the Haymarket, seems to have passed almost unnoticed; it was piously lachrymose and very dull.

In July came yet a third slim volume of poems, the title-piece being an *Ode to the Earl of Northumberland*; as well as odes to his fashionable friends, the book contained three lyrics with some very charming stanzas, for example, this foretaste of Wordsworth:

> Lo, thro' her works gay nature grieves
> How brief she is and frail,
> As ever o'er the falling leaves
> Autumnal winds prevail.
> Yet still the philosophic mind
> Consolatory food can find,

[1] This picture, originally in Madrid, now in the National Gallery, probably did not come to England before the Napoleonic Wars. It is not known where Smart could have seen a copy; perhaps his wife had one; perhaps in the trip abroad, of unknown date, mentioned in *Jubilate Agno*, D.42.

And hope her anchorage maintain:
We never are deserted quite;
'Tis by succession of delight
That love supports his reign.[1]

The lyrics won no praise: but the title-piece, a very tasteless thing spiced with a burst of anti-popery, caused the *Monthly* to lift its ban for a moment and write condescendingly: "For this Ode, however, he merits the thanks of every true Protestant, for he fights with a truly British spirit against the Whore of Babylon."

His final effort that year was a verse translation of *The Fables of Phaedrus*, commissioned by Dodsley, who had published his poems now that he had broken with Newbery and Carnan. It added nothing to his reputation either then or now, but it procured him some ready money which was what he desperately needed. Things were not going well with the much-advertised translation of the psalms. Charles Say who ran the *Gazetteer* had been announced as the printer, but he had been so scared by the poor sale of *A Song to David* that he had backed out, and no other printer seemed disposed to risk himself on Smart's behalf. Perhaps a good deal of the money advanced by subscription had already vanished. His friends, however—in this case his musical friends—remained loyal. A collection of forty-five melodies by twelve well-known organists including Boyce, Nares and Randall, was drawn up, corresponding to the different verse-forms used in his translation, and actually published in October 1765: *A Collection of Melodies for the Psalms of David According to the Version of Christopher Smart, M.A. By the most eminent Composers of Church Music.*

The announcement of this, earlier on, was not only a splendid advertisement; it was a sort of pledge (though in the event an unfulfilled one) that the version would be used in Church services and so command a good sale. Encouraged by this, the distinguished printer Dryden Leach accepted the task, and it went forward during 1765. Meanwhile Smart added to his sacred hymns one or two patriotic ones for the civic feasts of the Church of England.

Among Smart's sacred hymns is some of the most delicately

[1] "On a Bed of Guernsey Lilies."

sculptured verse he ever wrote. It is hard to read even the best of his psalm-paraphrases except as sketches for the *Song to David*. But the best of his hymns have a quality all their own, austerely tender, as if the baroque had developed gently and easily from the mediaeval, skipping the doubt and the passion and the grandeur that lay between, or as if Abelard's Latin had quite effortlessly become English, taking only a polish from the classics on the way. Perhaps the most beautiful are those for the feasts of Our Lord's infancy. Here are three stanzas on the Nativity:

> Where is this stupendous stranger,
> Swains of Solyma, advise,
> Lead me to my Master's manger,
> Shew me where my Saviour lies? . . .

> Spinks and ouzles sing sublimely,
> 'We too have a Saviour born,'
> Whiter blossoms burst untimely
> On the blest Mosaic thorn.

> God all-bounteous, all creative,
> Whom no ills from good dissuade,
> Is incarnate, and a native
> Of the very world he made.

What is so attractive about Smart's best poetry is the flush of enthusiasm caught with such lapidary precision. The last lines here are a compression into verse (whether intentional or not) of a prose sentence from the *De Nativitate* of Pope St Leo, himself a most concise and noble Latin-speaker:

> Deus omnipotens et clemens, cuius natura bonitas . . . cuius voluntas non potest sua benignitate privari . . . impassibilis, non dedignatus est homo esse passibilis, et immortalis mortis legibus subjacere.

Another lovely hymn is the May one to SS. Philip and James which contains this verse.

> Beeches, without order seemly,
> Shade the flow'rs of annua l birth,
> And the lily smiles supremely
> Mention'd by the Lord on earth.

There is also frequently a riddling element which gives

pleasure when the answer reveals itself—like the donkey in the second of these stanzas on the feast of the Presentation:

> I speak for all—for them that fly,
>   And for the race that swim;
> For all that dwell in moist and dry,
> Beasts, reptiles, flow'rs and gems to vie
>   When gratitude begins her hymn . . .
>
> By Jesus number'd all and priz'd,
>   Praise him in dale and hill;
> Ye beasts for use and peace devis'd,
> And thou which patient and despis'd,
>   Yet shalt a prophecy fulfill.

But the collection as a whole is uneven. Not infrequently he plunges into heated doggerel which is rather shocking by contrast:

> If we celebrate Matthias,
>   Let us do it heart and soul;
> Nor let worldly reasons bias
>   Our conceptions from their goal.
>
> As the fancy cools and rambles,
>   Keep her constant, keep her chaste:
> Ward from wine and from the shambles,
>   Sight and appetite, and taste.

There is also, especially in the civic hymns, the recurrent note of bitter anti-romanism:

> Her the hypocrites adore
>   In the fane of modern Rome,
> And from shadow's aid implore,
> That they may blaspheme the more,
>   And the more presume.

Smart's anti-romanism has already been mentioned more than once, and it may seem out of proportion to do so again. But I think—rightly or wrongly—that it is a most revealing symptom of his mental disorder. I do not think it can be passed off as the bluff exuberance of a good Church of England man. There is no sign of it in Smart before 1759; and it was not common among the contemporaries whose culture he shared—the Johnson circle for example. I think it points in two ways to the isolation and self-contradiction that was threatening his sanity: first, because it jarred with his own theology which, though eccentric, was more akin to Roman Catholicism than to current practice in the Church of England; secondly, because it was a symbol of his spoiled marriage.

It has already been remarked in what dangerous isolation his eccentric theology placed him, but I think it needs to be emphasized. If the Church of Rome was Anti-Christ, and if the Church of England continued (though he was still hoping strongly that it would not) to ignore him, he could only fall back deeper into that fatal pit of delusion: that he alone was right and all the rest of the world was wrong.

This threat to his sanity was made all the sharper by the inner contradiction concerning his wife. Sometimes, in the loneliness of his chastity, he was consoled by the conviction of his great mission; he had renounced his wife, firmly but compassionately, because she was "a Moabitish woman," an obstruction to his mission. But there were other times when he was shaken with spasms of wounded pride and anger; that it was really she who had deserted him and left him open to the powers of darkness. Whichever was nearer to the truth, it remains true that chastity becomes a deadly thing when it has to fall back for nourishment on anger and self-love.

But in the years 1764–5 he was still hoping for the official blessing of the Church of England on his psalms and hymns, which would send him forward with renewed faith. We have a splendidly detailed description of him at this time by Dr Hawkesworth, a close friend of Charles Burney, and a friend also of Smart's mother and sisters. Although deeply attached to Christopher, his mother and sisters felt a strong sympathy also with young Mrs Smart (Anna-Maria) in her efforts to build up a new life for herself and her daughters. Whether for that reason, or as part of a general renunciation of flesh and blood, Smart had quite cut himself off from them since his exodus from the asylum, Hawkesworth had been staying with Mrs Hunter and her mother (now very old and frail) at Margate, and they had begged him to call on Christopher and see how things stood. Hawkesworth's name is well known as author of the *Voyages Round the World* which incorporated Captain Cook's log-books and discovery of the new continent. But the great success of his volumes, when they came out in 1773, proved his undoing; for they excited so much jealousy and underhand calumny that—in spite of all his friends could do to distract and cheer him—he fell into a melancholy and died. Fanny Burney, then a young woman, in lamenting his death, couples his name with that of Smart, another of her elderly admirers: "victim of substantial as Dr Hawkesworth was that of shadowy disappointment."

Although it is a digression, it might be useful as well as amusing to have Fanny's picture of Hawkesworth before Hawkesworth's of Smart.

> I knew the voice of Dr Hawkesworth. He was engaged so deeply with Papa that neither seemed to know what they were about. However on coming into the parlour the Doctor made his compliments to me, and out of it they stalked again, and ran up into the study where they stayed some time, and then flying down the Doctor wished me goodnight, and got into the coach again, and Papa followed and talked with him at the door of it some time. There is an earnestness, a spirit in the conversation of very superior men which makes them absolutely forget every body and every thing about them, and which, when one knows not the subject which engages them, appears ridiculous to *spectators*; to *hearers* the appearance is different—I was only a spectator and could not possibly help laughing heartily to see them capering about all the time they talked as if they were bewildered. I believe it was only to look for books, and authors, and authorities for what they said.

Gentle, sensitive, fussy Dr Hawkesworth was just the right person to call and report on Christopher Smart. We can see the unfeigned joy and warmth with which he was received, we can see them "capering about" the book-lined study with the same "earnestness" observed by Miss Burney —then, suddenly, a blank shutter comes down when the family is mentioned. The conversation turns again to books and friends, and all is warmth and sparkle again—then, once more, for a moment the shutter descends. It is a sympathetic, conscientious description: we can make what we like of it.

> Dear Madam,
> I am afraid that you have before now secretly accused me, and I confess that appearances are against me; I did not however delay to

call on Mr Smart, but I was unfortunate enough twice to miss him. I was the third day of my being in town seized with a fever that was then epidemic, from which I am just but recovered. I have since my being in town this second time called on my old friend, and seen him. He received me with an ardour of kindness natural to the sensibility of his temper, and we were soon seated together by his fire side. I perceived upon his table a quarto book, in which he had been writing, a prayer book, and a Horace: after the first compliments, I said I had been at Margate, had seen his mother and sister, who expressed great kindness for him, and made me promise to come and see him; to this he made no reply; nor did he make any enquiry after those I mentioned; he did not even mention the place, nor ask me any questions about it, or what carried me thither. After some pause and some indifferent chat, I returned to the subject, and said that Mr Hunter and you would be very glad to see him in Kent: to this he replied very quick, "I cannot afford to be idle"; I said he might employ his mind as well in the country as in the town, at which he only shook his head; and I intirely changed the subject. Upon my asking him when we should see the Psalms, he said they were going to press immediately: as to his Other undertakings, I found he had compleated a translation of Phaedrus in verse for Dodsley at a certain price, and that he is now busy in translating all Horace into verse, which he sometimes thinks of publishing on his own account, and sometimes of contracting for it with a bookseller; I advised him to the latter, and he then told me he was in treaty about it, and believed it would be a bargain: he told me his principal motive for translating Horace into verse was to supersede the prose translation which he did for Newbery, which he said would hurt his memory. He intends however to review that translation, and print it at the foot of the page in his poetical version, which he proposes to print in quarto with the Latin, both in verse and prose, on the opposite page; he told me he once had thoughts of printing it by subscription, but as he had troubled his friends already, he was unwilling to do it again, and had been persuaded to publish it in numbers, which, though I rather dissuaded him, seemed at last to be the prevailing bent of his mind: he read me some of it: it is very close, and his own poetical fire sparkles in it very frequently; yet, upon the whole, it will scarcely take place of Francis's, and therefore, if it is not adopted as a school book, which perhaps may be the case, it will turn to little account. Upon mentioning his prose translation, I saw his countenance kindle, and snatching up the book, "What," says he, "do you think I had for this?" I said I could not tell. "Why," says he, with great indignation, "Thirteen pounds." I expressed very great astonishment, which he seemed to think he should increase by adding, "But, Sir, I gave a receipt for a hundred"; my astonishment however was now over, and I found that he had received only thirteen pounds because the rest had been advanced for his family; this was a tender point, and I found means immediately to divert him from it.

He is with very decent people, in a house most delightfully situated with a terras that overlooks St. James's Park, and a door into it. He was going to dine with an old friend of my own, Mr. Richard Dalton, who has an appointment in the King's library, and if I had not been particularly engaged, I would have dined with him. He had lately received a very genteel letter from Dr. Lowth, and is by no means considered in any light that makes his company as a gentleman, a scholar and a genius less desirable. I have been very particular, dear Madam, in relating all the particulars of this conference, that you may draw any inference, that I could draw from it, yourself.

I should incur my own censure, which is less tolerable than all others, if I did not express my sense of the civilities I received from you and Mrs Hunter, while I was at Margate: I have Mrs. Hawkesworth's express request in a letter now before me to do the same on her part: if you, or any of the family, come into our part of the country, we shall be very glad to accomodate you with a table and a bed; you will find a chearful fire-side and a hearty welcome. If in the mean time I can do you any series of pleasure here, you will the more oblige as you the more freely command me.

Our best compliments attend you, Mr Hunter, your young gentleman, and Mrs. Smart, not forgetting the ladies we met at your house, particularly one who I think is daughter to Mrs Holmes.

> I am,
>> Madam,
>> Your obedient humble servant,
>>> JOHN HAWKESWORTH.

LONDON, Oct. 1764.

One thing at any rate is pretty clear from this letter. There is no truth in the impression conveyed by some writers that Smart was a habitual drunkard. He was not, says Hawkesworth, considered in any light that made his company as a scholar, a gentleman and a genius less desirable; and this is confirmed by his verse-epistle to Dr. Nares, the musician—he was in the habit of writing his invitations or thanks to his friends in verse—which ends:

> P.S. I have (don't think it a chimaera)
> Some good sound Port and right Madeira.

A drunkard would not write about drink in that casual and friendly manner.

Very vivid, and very puzzling, is the brusque "I cannot afford to be idle!"—and the refusal even to inquire after his mother and sister. The more puzzling because his references in *Jubilate Agno* to mother and to nephew—the "young gentleman" of Hawkesworth's letter, who wrote the memoir of 1791—are affectionate and quite free from bitterness. My explanation is that Smart consciously cut himself off from them because of the Gospel text, "He that leaveth not father and mother . . . cannot be my disciple"; but that there was also an unprobed, irrational groundswell of bitterness—not for any wrong they had done him, but just a revulsion against memories of dependence, against "the Cradle." The same kind of bitterness, though not so sharp, as that against his wife; for—in the lines on "the Cradle" in *Jubilate Agno*—he included the infirmities of childhood with weakness of the flesh in general.

The outburst against Newbery, which Hawkesworth noted, was against dependence of another kind, monetary dependence. Here again, in *Jubilate Agno*, he had shown no bitterness when he heard that Newbery was sponsoring James Merrick's translation of the psalms; Merrick, after all, was a clergyman of Reading, well known to the Newbery and Carnan families. But that was when Smart was expecting his version to be out in 1763; when it was postponed for a year, and then for another year, and Merrick's seemed likely to come out first after all, perhaps panic at the thought of failure stirred the sour sediment within him. All his modern biographers (except Mr Brittain) say that he was obsessed by the mania that everyone was in league to persecute him. But the truer thing to say is that he always had *to fight against this obsession*.

As to the pain which his attitude caused his mother and sister, we can read it easily between the lines of a letter which Mrs Hunter wrote to young Mrs Smart; she preserved it, and it passed from her descendants into the care of the Reading Public Library. Old Mrs Smart died not long after the reception of Hawkesworth's letter—in 1765 or 1766. Mrs Hunter wrote to Anna-Maria, care of Mr Newbery's lodgings, to be forwarded to her at Reading where she had been managing the family paper since 1762.

Margate May 8th

My Dear Sister
    I am very sorry that after so long an interval, I should renew our correspondence on a melancholy occasion, but I owe it to the tender

respect which I shall always bear you, for your many actions towards me of affectionate and friendly regard, to inform you that it has pleased God to take our poor Mother to his Mercy out of this scene of sorrow and disappointment, for such it has been to her on many sad accounts; she departed Last night at about a quarter past 8. There is a paper in her own handwriting giving order about her Funeral. Six of the poorest Widows of the place are to be pall bearers to have each a stuff Gown, to be saved out of the price of the Coffin, which is to be a very mean one, besides these we are ordered to make no invitations, but this day's post carries a Letter to my Brother to tell him if he thinks of coming to the Bur[y]ing he must be at Margate by next Tuesday night. God bless you and yours, my dear sister, with every Happiness that does indeed deserve the name. I hope you and I shall see each other again in this World, if not I humbly trust we shall meet in the Blissful Regions of Love, Harmony, and ever-lasting Friendship,

Yours truly affectionate
M. HUNTER.

The unclouded affection between Margaret Hunter and Anna-Maria Smart speaks for itself.

It is not known whether Christopher did attend the burying of his mother, of whom he had written:

> For I am the seed of the WELCH WOMAN and speak the truth from my heart.

THIRTEEN

Failure and Isolation

ALTHOUGH Smart had spoken confidently to Hawkesworth in October 1764 about the imminent appearance
of the psalms and hymns, there was a further delay of nearly
a year. "The heart grows sick with hope deferred." Merrick's
appeared first. Smart had probably taken part of the force
of the blow that was coming to him when his own appeared.

It was to be expected that he would get no joy from his
enemies of the *Monthly* and the *Critical*, but even they went
beyond any limit they had previously reached in contemp-
tuous denigration. The *Monthly* of September 1765 gave six
laudatory pages to Merrick's translation, then turned to
Smart with the single comment that

> Some unhappy circumstances in this gentleman's life seem to have
> given his later writings a peculiar claim to a total exemption from
> criticism. Accordingly we chuse to be silent with regard to the merit
> of the present publication.

The *Critical*, less barbed but more brutal, used Smart merely
as a foil for Merrick and concluded:

> The reader will undoubtedly be glad to find that the Psalmist is at
> last delivered from a crowd of wretched poets, who had overwhelmed
> his native grace and dignity under the rubbish of their despicable
> schemes: the admirers of these beautiful compositions may read
> them with pleasure in Mr. Merrick's translations.

This indeed, though not expressed so cruelly, was the general
verdict, and posterity in the next generation or two endorsed
it. Merrick's biographer tells us that "his paraphrases were

in extensive use both in the Church of England and with the Nonconformists in the early part of this [the nineteenth] century," and at least one of his hymns—"The Festal Morn, O God, is come"—is still sung in Congregational churches. But the name of Christopher Smart is quite unknown in any hymn-book or prayer-book. His daughter Elizabeth seems to have been the only person until the present century to see any beauty in his hymns; she could not manage the *Song to David*, but she loved the best of his hymns and had them published along with her own pleasant poems in 1826.

It was this complete ignoring of him by the Church of England—not the barbs of his adversaries—that was the real blow to Smart. Even before his confinement, and increasingly after it, he had sought to interest church dignitaries on his behalf. Hawkesworth noted the "genteel answer" he had received from Dr Lowth. Lowth was the author of the book on Hebrew poetry (1743) which had greatly influenced Smart. In that year, 1765, he was being savagely belaboured by Warburton, Bishop of Gloucester (whom Smart had attacked sharply in his verses to Dr. Webster when he was a young man);[1] but in the following year Lowth got his bishopric, St David's. "A genteel letter" seems as far as he was prepared to go in Smart's favour.

Warburton, in spite of his brilliance, represented the golden and persistent mean of official Anglicanism. He would have had no use for Smart. Neither would the progressive elements of that time which were later to coalesce into the Evangelical movement; Cowper, if anyone, was the poet of their predilection. These elements were twofold: those clergymen who were sympathizing increasingly with John Wesley, and those that frequented the drawing-room at Chelsea or the Chapel at Bath of Selina, Countess of Huntingdon, who "appointed such persons to officiate as ministers as she thought fit, revoking such appointments at her pleasure." With these rival potentates ("Pope John" and

---

[1] Warburton's enormous footnotes were likened to places of execution where anyone who had had the temerity to disagree with him received public chastisement.

"Pope Joan" as they were rudely called) Smart had nothing in common.

As has been said before, the only divine whose theology —from internal evidence—seems to have been mainly congenial was William Law. But Law had died a lonely eccentric with only two disciples, women. After his *Serious Call to a Devout and Holy Life* (1728), which established him as the best spiritual writer in England, he found himself increasingly drawn to writers of the Church of Rome, both pre- and post-reformation; in fact he could find nothing wrong with that church, he said, except its claims to temporal power and persecution. Then abruptly he turned aside and plunged into the strange theosophizing of Jacob Boehme; his works after that were barren as far as an effective apostolate was concerned.

There is a certain parallel with the life of Smart. Smart seemed to have been moving along the same Anglo-Catholic lines as the Oxford thinkers of the next century: lines which led Newman to face the sudden dilemma that the Church of Rome was either true or it was anti-Christ. Smart decided that it was anti-Christ. At the same time came his mental breakdown, and then his eccentric development of the branch theory: that the Church of England was the Catholic Church of the West, and St Paul's, London, was to take the place of St Peter's, Rome. This eccentricity isolated him as effectively as "Boehmenism" isolated Law. He was probably very muddled about his own future, but he was clear in his mind that the first step would be official approval of his psalms and hymns.

Not long before he left confinement he had had a mental vision, "The Lord magnify the idea of Smart singing hymns on this day in the eyes of the whole University of Cambridge. Nov. 5th. 1762. N.S." But what faced him in fact in November 1765 was the Debtors' Prison. Not long after the publication of his *Translation of the Psalms* his printer, Dryden Leach, had him arrested for a debt of £86.

It looks as if a good number of the 700 subscribers had failed to claim their copies—and to pay the other half of their subscriptions. One of these apparently was John Sharp, then

Archdeacon of Northumberland, one of the numerous clerics whom Smart had hoped to enlist on his side. The news of Smart's plight comes in a letter to the Archdeacon from Granville Sharp, the philanthropist, who was at that time working in the Ordnance Department in the City of London. Granville's letter, hitherto unpublished, is another interesting example of Smart's appeal to men of intellect and sensibility, though this time there was the additional link of Durham. The letter is dated "3 Jan. 1766":

> A few days ago I received a letter from Mr. Smart desiring directions where to send the 10 Books of his Psalms for which you subscribed, and signifying that he had been arrested by his Printer for £86, and that he "must have finished an unfortunate life in jail had it not been for the good nature of a Friend, who could not bear to see his tears."—In return I desired him to send the Books to me (which I have since received) and said I would take your directions for the disposal of them; so please to inform me in your next, how you will have them sent.
>
> I wish some kind of place, or employment, could be found for poor Smart; surely he must be very capable of earning a comfortable subsistence, if he was but put in the way of it.[1]

The letter is also evidence of the depth of the wound Smart had received; for, in spite of all his previous vicissitudes, this is the first known instance of his breaking down in public.

Because of the intervention of the generous "Friend" who paid the £86, there is no public record of Smart's arrest. But there is confirmation of it in another of Smart's letters— the first of an interesting series recently discovered and published in the *Review of English Studies*, May 1957. They were written to a Welshman, Paul Panton, of Plâs Gwyn, Anglesey, and Holywell, Flintshire, who had been a pensioner at Trinity Hall in 1744 and remained one of Smart's wide circle of faithful friends. It is dated 10 January 1766 from "Storey's Gate Coffee House, St. James's Park." It relates his arrest by the printer for £86 and his rescue by a kind friend, and ends with an appeal for help towards yet another volume of

[1] For knowledge of this letter and a copy of it I am much indebted to Mr John A. Woods, and to the owner, Miss Lloyd-Baker of Hardwicke Court, Gloucester, for permission to publish it.

his *Miscellaneous Poems*. There is no clue as to the identity of the friend who saved him. The *Miscellaneous Poems* were advertised in his verse translation of Horace, but never published, and no trace of them remains. It was probably for them that Smart was appealing in another begging letter addressed to George Colman the playwright, dated "Febry the 27th 1766" from "St James's Park next door to the Cockpit".

Sir,
I find myself reduced by the necessity of the case again to tax such of my friends as are disposed to do me the honour of their names,
I am with much respect,
Your obliged Servant
CHRISTOPHER SMART.

A year later, another letter to Paul Panton, the second of the series (22 January 1767), shows Smart in a much better position. Two friends, Mr. Mason, now a King's Chaplain, and Mr. Stonhewer,[1] his old companion of Durham and Pembroke, had set him up.

Mason, the good-hearted busybody, who had no interest in Smart's poetry but much in his welfare, had put his popularity on a business footing by organizing an annual guinea subscription (a sort of "Save Smart" fund) among his friends. Stonhewer had become private secretary to the Duke of Grafton, the Prime Minister of 1766, who had been his pupil at Cambridge; he had managed to get Smart on the list of Expectants for a Poor Knight of Windsor. This was a sort of lay canonry which brought an annuity with it. It is confirmed by the *Domestic Entry Book* for 26 April 1766, which notes that the King intended to accord Smart the next place of Poor Chevalier which should become vacant in the Chapel of St George. The vacancy did not in fact occur, but it was almost certainly Stonhewer who procured for Smart a pension of £50 a year from the Treasury.

Not only the money but even more the recognition must have been a wonderful encouragement for him. If it was not

[1] Often written "Stonehewer," but he always called himself "Stonhewer."

exactly official recognition, it was next door to official. It revived his hopes for his psalms and hymns. His third letter to Paul Panton a month later (12 February 1767) is a rather pathetic request that copies of his *Translation of the Psalms* which are not wanted in Wales be sent back to London, for he feels they are wanted there.

Thus the year 1767 saw a new lease of life for Smart. But the horror of the Debtors' Prison which he had so narrowly—and almost miraculously—escaped in December 1765 had been a severe shock to him. "Shades of the prison house" continued to haunt him and to play upon his nerves. His despised enemy "The Purse" had caught up with him. In confinement, his old light-hearted attitude to money had made "The Purse" seem the least formidable of the three. "The Cradle"—abstinence from women—and "The Coffin"—deprivation of his liberty—he had managed to survive. But now "The Purse" had returned with a vengeance. Money and the need for money became his constant care.

The verse translation of Horace mentioned by Hawkesworth was probably completed before the shock of December 1765. It appeared with the revival of Smart's fortunes early in 1767 in four very handsome volumes dedicated to Sir Francis Blake Delaval, brother of the Lord Delaval who had been his pupil at Cambridge. Both the translation and Smart's preface to it are of great interest as showing his complete sanity and urbanity in everything that did not probe the one secret obsession.

No detailed criticism of the translation can be expected here. It is extremely hard to come by; a commercial failure—as Hawkesworth had anticipated—it has never been reprinted; the two-volume "Muses" edition of 1949 understandably had no room for it. Further, to criticize a verse rendering of Horace is a rigorously specialist task. But it does seem true to say that it is a triumph of talent and industry. He was especially concerned to catch the *curiosa felicitas* of Horace. Mr Brittain quotes his rendering of *Difficile est proprie communia dicere*:

> 'Tis arduous common things to say
> In such a clean peculiar way
> Until they fairly seem your own.

"Peculiar" is Smart's favourite adjective for subtleties (e.g. "And quick peculiar quince"), as "stupendous" is for mysteries. If one turns, as a rusty Latinist, to the famous *simplex munditiis* passage one finds this very satisfying rendering:

> Pyrrha, for whom with such an air
> Do you bind back your golden hair?
> So seeming in your cleanly vest,
> Whose plainness is the pink of taste—

Lines like the following—the beginning and end of the Ode to Torquatus—will emphasize the irony that his prose crib of 1756 still lingers on while his verse translation has altogether fled:

> The melted snow the verdure now restores,
>   And leaves adorn the trees;
> The season shifts—subsiding to their shores
>   The rivers flow with ease.
> The Grace, with nymphs and with her sisters twain,
>   Tho' naked dares the dance—
> That here's no permanence the years explain,
>   And days, as they advance . . .
>
> When you shall die, tho' Minos must acquit
>   A part so nobly played;
> Race, eloquence, and goodness, from the pit
>   Cannot restore your shade.
> For nor Diana's heavenly power or love
>   Hippolytus revives;
> Nor Theseus can Perithous remove
>   From his Lethean gyves.

The translation was a test of his talent, not his genius. But in the preface to the translation he showed that creative genius was still what profoundly interested him and that creative inspiration was still for him childed by heavenly wisdom and the Divine Word. Discussing Horace's *curiosa felicitas*, he suddenly switches to the more profound source of poetry:

Besides the *Curiosa Felicitas*, so much of Horace by himself, there is another poetical excellence, which tho' possessed in a degree by every great genius, is exceeding in our Lyric to surpass; I mean the beauty, force, and vehemence of *Impression*: which leads me on to a rare and entertaining subject, not anywhere (I think) insisted on by others.

Impression, then, is a talent or gift of Almighty God, by which a Genius is empowered to throw an emphasis on a word or a sentence in such wise, that it cannot escape any reader of sheer good sense, and true critical sagacity. This power will sometimes keep it up thro' the medium of a prose translation; especially in scripture, for in justice to truth and everlasting pre-eminence, we must confess this virtue to be far more powerful and abundant in the sacred writings.

Smart then gives some examples from scripture in Hebrew and English, but they are not very enlightening. The brief but brilliant illumination sputters out after two paragraphs. It is one of the most tantalizing descriptions we have by a "maker" of his own "making"—enlarging as it does on the lines in *Jubilate Agno*:

For my talent is to give an impression upon words by punching, that when the reader casts his eye upon 'em, he takes up the image from the mould wch I have made.

But I do not think it is wise to rationalize it more than Smart himself has done. His intuitions are valuable, but his reasoning was weak. When disturbed from his contemplation he was too liable to be snared by petty distractions.[1]

The preface—as opposed to the translation—was probably written after the shock of near-imprisonment, for he concludes unexpectedly with the complaint that:

a gentleman derived from ancestors who have abode upon their own Lordship six hundred years in the County Palatine of Durham, should have been reduced in a manner by necessity to a work of this kind, which if done in a state he had more reason to be satisfied with, had been more likely to have given satisfaction.

This note of whining arrogance is something new in Smart.

[1] Mr Brittain gives an example—the lines from *A Song to David*:

> For ADORATION beasts embark,
> While waves upholding halcyon's ark
> No longer roar and toss.

The *Monthly* reviewer of the first edition condescendingly noted that there *was* supposed to be "a certain large quadruped that uses a piece of timber to prey upon fish." In the second edition Smart hastily accepted this fatuous suggestion and added a footnote to that effect.

"The Purse" was haunting him. The ancestral home of Snotterton to which he was heir (though his cousin Francis had mortgaged it heavily) was evidently in his mind as a possible means of restoring his finances.

In December of that year, 1767, John Newbery died. One-third of his estate was to be held in trust for Anna-Maria by her brother and half-brother with two provisions: "that the receipt alone of the said Anna-Maria Smart shall from time to time be a sufficient discharge to my said son for what she shall receive of him"; and that "the same or any part thereof shall not be subject to the debt, power or control of her present husband." The *Reading Mercury*—run by "Anna-Maria Smart and Company" since 1762—was now entering on a period of vigorous expansion. It was about this time that she sent her daughters, aged fourteen and fifteen, to be educated at a convent in France; this fact is known from a manuscript reminiscence of the Reading (Catholic) Mission 1752–1840, written by her grand-daughter; the beginning alone is relevant here:

> In the year 1762 my Grandmother, Anna Maria Smart, was sent to Reading by her relations to take the management of the then sole County Newspaper, the long established "Reading Mercury." She was the widow of the unfortunate poet, Christopher Smart, well known to the chief literary men of that period. On her own side, she was the descendant of respectable Catholic ancestry, and like her progenitors adhered to the Faith through all the obloquy and insult attached, at that time and long after, to its name and exercise.
>
> In defiance of the reproachful wonder of her Protestant Patrons, Mrs Smart sent her daughters, Marianne and Elizabeth to the Ursuline Convent at Boulogne-sur-Mer, where they remained three years. In this asylum of peace and innocence was laid the solid groundwork of religion which endured through all the moral trials, hardly conceivable in these less ignorant, and therefore less bigoted days, which beset their early youth. These first impressions lasted to the end of their career, as did their filial love for their first holy teachers.[1]

The rest of the manuscript describes Mrs Smart's devoted services to the French *emigrés* (one of whom, the Chevalier

[1] The original MS perished in air-raids on Portsmouth, but a transcript had been made by Archbishop King, who kindly sent me a copy. I have altered "1752" in the transcript to "1762" since that is known to be the correct date.

Jean de la Brousse le Noir, married Elizabeth in 1795) and her establishment of a Roman Catholic chapel in the town of Reading.

What angers, what envy, what regrets, were stirred in Smart when he came to hear about the will and about Polly and Bess going to a foreign convent, we do not know. He did not lay aside his bitterness against Rome until a year before his death.

He was still writing busily, but his gift of "Impression" had well nigh deserted him. In 1768 came another oratorio, *Abimelech*, a doleful piece of no distinction; and then a more considerable effort, all the parables of Christ, along with many other Gospel scenes, turned into rhyming couplets— well over 3,000 lines. It is a most meritorious work, straight-forward and thoughtful. He evidently hoped that it would be taken up by parents and teachers, and that children would learn to prattle easily the gospel story:

> Christ Jesus on a certain day
> Upon a mountain went to pray,
> Commanding Peter to be there,
> And John and James to join in pray'r . . .

It might well have succeeded. At least one can imagine it catching on in Sunday Schools a century later. But in fact it was never reprinted and, like all his later works, passed into oblivion. The occasional outburst against Rome occurs as in the lesser hymns. The parable of the foolish virgins ends—ironically, considering his daughters—

> Wretches like these would all to *Rome*
> And go to them that sell perfume,
> And to the *man of sin* apply,
> There pardons and indulgence buy:
> But Christ against the fools, that put
> Their trust in man, his door has shut.

Christ's promise to Peter of the headship of the Church which will never fail is cleverly turned by linking it with the subsequent scene in which Peter is rebuked: "Get thee behind me, Satan."

> But Jesus bade the devil recede,
> Or Peter had been Pope indeed.

Most of his publications since 1763 had been commercial failures. They must have injured rather than helped his finances. They certainly made him increasingly distrusted by the printers and booksellers, who had to bear most of the loss. Apart from his £50 pension he now had only Mason's subscription-scheme to rely on. A letter to Paul Panton—one of many, probably, of the same sort to others—of 4 January 1768 shows what a nerve-racking business this was for Smart; he reminds Panton that this is "the Anniversary of Mason's kind plan" and begs him to continue his two guineas a year. Panton not only did so, but, to save Smart embarrassment, asked a London friend, Wynne, to pay it on his account next year without being asked. It is a small example of the malicious fortune that now seemed to be dogging Smart that Wynne, through some confusion, failed to pay it in time; and Smart had to write again with pathetic urgency in January 1769.

This letter, the last of the series to Panton, reveals what may well have been the final calamity for Smart, the *coup de grace* to his earthly hopes. His cousin, Francis Smart, the head of the family, to whom Christopher was heir-at-law, had died and left him nothing in his will. Francis had died in August or September 1768; his will, signed 11 August, was probated 26 September. The name of Christopher was not mentioned in it. But the letter to Panton shows him still clinging to the belief that he was entitled to something. It is dated 2 January 1769, from Storey's Gate, St. James's Park:

> I send this for the favour of your annual two guineas, which I am in want of, God knows: tho' by the death of Frank Smart I am direct heir to an Estate of six hundred pounds a year. But so obstinate is my adversity that a thousand obstacles are thrown in the way of my just claim.

Francis's estate consisted of certain lands and tenements in Sussex which he held jointly with a lawyer called Boughey. By his will of August 1768 his share was to be sold to Boughey and the proceeds divided among Richard Smart, attorney of Staple Inn, Louisa Smart, and John Smart—a minor—when he should come of age. The sale realized the sum of £630, but this of course was capital, not income.

A few months later, 29 July 1769, Christopher was obliged to sign a tripartite indenture affirming that his position as heir-at-law gave him no claim on Francis's estate. The three parties were: (1) George Boughey who had bought Francis's share of the Sussex properties for £630; (2) Richard Smart, who received the £630 for himself and for Louisa Smart; neither of these Smarts is described as being any relation of Francis, though presumably they were second cousins; and (3) "Christopher Smart of Chelsea . . . Cousin and Heir at law of the said Francis Smart, that is to say, the son of Peter Smart who was the Younger Brother of John Smart who was the father of the said Francis Smart." For his part in signing this quittance Christopher Smart received from George Boughey the nominal sum of five shillings.

Although Christopher laid no claim to Francis's personal estate, he remained quite convinced that the ancestral house and lands on Staindrop Moor ought to descend to him as heir at law and next of kin. It is not unlikely that he borrowed money on the strength of his conviction. The Snotterton deeds, which are among the Vane papers at Raby Castle, show that although the place was heavily mortgaged there were still some hundreds of pounds to be got out of it.

The story told by the deeds is as follows. The original property had passed in succession to the Smart next of kin "and his heirs forever" since 1629. In 1753 Francis, Christopher's cousin, inherited it from his father John. In January 1758 he mortgaged it for three thousand pounds. In July 1763 he raised a further loan on it of £1,053. By this time he was living in London, at Grays Inn, and dealing in real estate in Sussex. At his death in 1768 he had done nothing to redeem the house and lands of Snotterton, though he had paid the interest to date. His will of August 1768 made no actual mention of Snotterton but simply left all his estates to Richard and Louisa Smart to be sold and the proceeds divided between them. Lord Darlington, on whose lands the property bordered, offered to pay off the total mortgage of £4,053, plus six months' interest that was outstanding, and then to buy the house and lands for the sum of £647.

On 17 January 1770 a tripartite indenture to this effect was drawn up between Richard and Louisa Smart, "Christopher Smart of Chelsea," and the Earl of Darlington. There were three seals, but only two signatures, Richard's and Louisa's— not Christopher's. The £647 was to be paid to Richard and Louisa; Christopher was to receive, as before, only the nominal sum of five shillings. In the text of the indenture it is said that Richard and Louisa, in spite of anything done by Francis's ancestors, "do now have good right and power and lawful and absolute authority to convey the same manor to the Earl of Darlington." A little later, 29 January, there is a further deed saying that this has been done. Once more "Christopher Smart of Chelsea" is mentioned as "cousin and heir at law"; but once more, though there are three seals, his signature is missing.

Either he was not to be found at that time (though he was still at liberty), or else, more probably, he was still standing on the plaintive claim he had made in his letter to Paul Panton of January 1769, "by the death of Frank Smart I am direct heir to an Estate of six hundred pounds a year. But . . . a thousand obstacles are thrown in the way of my just claim."

Christopher's claim would certainly have been a just one if the property had been entailed. But there seems no sort of probability that such was the case. The phrase "and his heirs forever" which occurs in various Smart wills is not enough by itself to show an entail, and the description "heir at law" means merely the person entitled to succeed to land in the event of an intestacy. Moreover, if there had been an entail, Francis Smart would have had only a life interest and, therefore, could not lawfully have mortgaged the freehold. Under those circumstances the mortgagees would hardly have advanced him £4,000, which seems to have been about 80 per cent of the property's value. If, then, there was no entail, Christopher had no legal right to Snotterton, since the owner had willed all his estates to Richard and Louisa.

On the other hand, it was not a sign of any special imbecility on his part that he *thought* he had a just claim. It was a mistake that might very easily be made; for, in the eyes of the ordinary law, the heir at law *was* the person entitled to the property. The Statute of Wills of 1540 gave a man freedom for the first time to include real property in his will; but it did not provide for an executor. Consequently, the land was still legally inherited by the heir, just as personal property was by the executor. But if the heir tried to take it for himself, a Court of Equity would intervene and compel him to convey it in accordance with the will. This state of affairs lasted till the Land Transfer Act of 1897 by which both real and personal property passed to the executor; after this no more was heard of the heir at law.

Christopher's mistake about his rights as heir at law went back as far as August 1759 when he was entering the private madhouse and was persuaded, according to his own account, to "make over his inheritance". Here is the full passage which was referred to briefly in chapter 8:

> Let Phuvah rejoice with Platycerotes,[1] whose weapons of defence keep them innocent.
> For I this day made over my inheritance to my mother in consideration of her infirmities.
> Let Shimron rejoice with the Kite, who is of more value than many sparrows.
> For I this day made over my inheritance to my mother in consideration of her age.
> Let Sered rejoice with the Wittal[2]—a silly bird is wise unto his own preservation.
> For I this day made over my inheritance to my mother in consideration of her poverty.
> Let Elon rejoice with Attelabus, who is the Locust without wings.
> For I bless the thirteenth of August, in which I had the grace to obey the voice of Christ in my conscience.
> Let Jahleel rejoice with the Woodcock, who liveth upon suction and is pure from his diet.
> For I bless the thirteenth of August, in which I was willing to run all hazards for the sake of the name of the Lord.
> Let Shuni rejoice with the Gull, who is happy in not being good for food.
> For I bless the thirteenth of August, in which I was willing to be called a fool for the sake of Christ.

The continued references to cuckoldry, here and elsewhere in this part of *Jubilate Agno*, give the drift of the altercation at least as it appeared to Christopher Smart. He would have

---

[1] *Platycerotes*: stags with broad horns.
[2] *Wittal*, or wittol, used for a cuckold or a half-wit.

protested that the ancestral manor should descend to him and his heirs for ever. His cousins in reply would have pointed out the unlikelihood of his producing a male heir since his wife had left him.

It must be accepted—Smart's assertions are so emphatic—that his signature was really required by his cousins for some document in August 1759. But for what sort of document we do not know. Perhaps it was in connection with the mortgaging of Snotterton by Francis Smart. Somewhere, in some dusty sack, it may still survive, dated 13 August 1759, featuring "Christopher Smart of Chelsea" the heir at law, as in the later documents, in receipt of the nominal sum of five shillings.

In all the later documents, beginning with that of July 1769, his address is given as Chelsea. Yet as late as January 1769 it was still Storey's Gate in Westminster. Admittedly the obvious inference is that between January and July he changed his address. But when the form "Christopher Smart of Chelsea" is found on the documents of 1770 which he did not sign, a conjecture arises and persists that the address has simply been copied from the earlier documents of 1769, and that that in turn had been copied from the still earlier, hypothetical document of August 1759—when his address might indeed have been, according to Mrs Thrale's reminiscence, the private lodgings in Chelsea.

The blow to Smart in the Snotterton affair was one more instance of his old enemy "the Purse" taking revenge. In confinement he had rejoiced over his supposed renunciation of his inheritance: "For my grounds in New Canaan shall infinitely compensate me for the flats and maynes of Staindrop Moor."

But after his release in 1763 his views seem to have changed and "the Purse" began to haunt him. This, however, was its last blow. As the next chapter shows, it was the prelude to his final acceptance of "willing poverty."

FOURTEEN

———◈———

"*We never are deserted quite*"

IT may have been a cause or only a coincidence, but after the affair of Frank Smart's will nothing more is heard—with one or two exceptions—of Christopher's friends and patrons. They seem to have decided "Poor Kit is finished. There is nothing more to be done for him." At the same time he had to put more and more of a strain on himself to preserve the externals of sanity.

A revealing picture of him is given by Fanny Burney, then aged sixteen, in her diary of 14 September 1768:

> Mr Smart the poet was here yesterday. . . . This ingenious writer is one of the most unfortunate of men—he has been twice confined in a madhouse—and but last year sent a most affecting epistle to Papa, to entreat him to lend him half a guinea!—How great a pity so clever, so ingenious a man should be reduced to such shocking circumstances. He is extremely grave, and has still great wildness in his manner, looks, and voice; but 'tis impossible to *see* him, and to *think* of his works, without feeling the utmost concern for him.

The phrases "extremely grave" and "great wildness," coming from this quick-witted and tender-hearted girl, tell their own story of hidden conflict and disorder.

Fanny's father, Dr Charles Burney, was one of the very few—perhaps the only one—of his old friends who continued to help him to the end. Others, like the great-hearted Granville Sharp, were still concerned about him; James Sharp wrote to the Archdeacon on 10 February 1769:

> Granville also desires I will tell you that poor Kit Smart has been with him, desiring that you will not forget the Charity he has had of £10 from the Trustees, he says it is of great consequence to him.[1]

[1] These were the Trustees of Lord Crewe.

But of the hundreds of friends who had rallied to help him after his release we now hear no more.

This letter, dated 1769, from a man called Shaw, was perhaps typical of many who were abandoning him:

> I beg your pardon for having troubled you with a letter relative to Mr Smart whose pretensions, I am since informed, are merely visionary, and indeed from that and other circumstances, I am led to believe he still retains something of his former insanity. I have withdrawn from him for some weeks past.

With the falling-away of friends went the last surety that could persuade printers and booksellers to risk themselves on his behalf. But it was not only his friends' confidence in him that was wavering, it was his own confidence in himself. The castle of his self-persuasion was being cracked wide open at last.

On the strength of his divinely appointed mission he had levied subscriptions on all his friends and with the money thus supplied had poured out about 100,000 words of fervid piety in verse. About one per cent of that output was imperishable poetry; the remainder was just words upon words about the practice of piety—not backed up by any particular deed to show their validity. It is not to be doubted that in his first conversion and during his confinement he had many moments of profound union with God and of genuine sustentation by divine grace. But in his writings 1764–8 I can find only one instance of the healing peace that piety should bring, and that is not in any of the sacred poems; it is in a sad and lovely secular lyric:

> We never are deserted quite;
> 'Tis by succession of delight
> That love supports his reign.

Meanwhile the vicious circle was inexorably coming round to its starting-point. Levies on his friends and his own ceaseless stream of print had seemed justified by his divine mission. But in fact it was the other way round. Without the help of his friends, without the ceaseless self-persuasion of print, the conviction of his divine mission began to crack and crumble. It must have been shockingly painful, for he had lived with it and on it for thirteen years.

But the wonderful thing about Smart—the thing, if one may say so without impertinence, that makes his life worth writing—is that in his very failure and collapse he was able to vindicate God's goodness and mercy as never before.

In the falling-away of friends and printers, one person came forward to help him. That was his brother-in-law, Thomas Carnan. All that we know of Carnan, apart from his work for Newbery, is his stubborn resistance to the Stationers Company over a question of monopoly (it is said that he always carried a spare shirt around with him in case of sudden arrest). He was a good craftsman and a hard fighter. It seems likely—though there can be no certainty—that the impulse which turned him back to Smart, in spite of all that had intervened, came from his sister Anna-Maria. Carnan, with great tact, approached him indirectly. In a letter of 16 April 1769—and between its lines—can be read Smart's first painful struggle to free himself from the interior straitjacket of his pseudo-messiahship.

Dear Sir,
   Being informed by Mr Leach & afterwards by Messrs Mason and Stonhewer that you have determined very benevolently in my favour, I think it incumbent on me to be thankful, Indeed if mercy be not shown me somewhere or other I do not see how I can possibly escape a prison. I congratulate you therefore upon your kind resolution, as you may depend upon it that it will not only be finally a great thing for yourself, but people even now will applaud your generosity and good nature. I desire my duty to Mrs Newbery & will wait on you or give you the meeting when & where you will please to name.
                        Yours most sincerely
                           and affectionately,
                              CHRISTOPHER SMART.

The background to this letter is evidently that Leach (perhaps his former printer) told him: I can do nothing for you, but Carnan has said that he would print for you again if you asked him. Mason and Stonhewer, also, who had done all they could for five years and were anxious to be quit of him in the kindest possible manner, said: Your brother-in-law is anxious to arrange a meeting with you, and he is the one who can best help you now.

What is interesting about the letter is the way it changes, as it goes on, from awkward dignity to simple friendship. With its greeting to his mother-in-law Mrs Newbery who lived with Carnan, it is the first instance since 1762 of an affectionate word or gesture from Smart towards his family. Although its occasion was his own want, I do not think it is an example of needy opportunism. Its tone is strongly suggestive of severe self-questioning and genuine hard-won humility. I would guess that it is a date in his spiritual history quite as important as that of his conversion in 1756.

With the liberation from his interior strait-jacket there vanished that strain which he had been putting on himself to live up to his own idea of himself. There was a return of his old lighthearted gaiety, accompanied now by a relaxed and gentle melancholy. From Fanny Burney again comes one of the last descriptions of him—on a Friday some time in October or November 1769: "Poor Mr Smart presented me this morning with a rose, blooming and sweet as if we were in the month of June. 'It was given me,' said he, 'by a fair lady—though not so fair as *you*!' I have always admired *poetical* license! . . . This, however, is nothing to what he afterwards amused himself by saying." She was nursing wounded literary aspirations herself at this time; so she has harsh words for the *Critical* reviewers who had slandered Smart and who would have sent him to a madhouse for a third time, she says, "If they heard that he had descended to flatter and praise *me*! even little me, F.B., or Q. in a corner." This sounds a different Smart from the one of September 1768 who was "extremely grave" and had a "great wildness in his manner, looks, and voice."

Another picture of him at this time is quoted by Mr Brittain from a memoir of John Kempe (born 1748) who had great skill as a flute-player: "Smart loved to hear me play upon my flute, and I have often soothed the wanderings of his melancholy by some favourite air; he would shed tears when I played, and generally wrote some lines afterwards."

Here are some of the lines which music helped him to write:

O pluck me quick the raven's quill,
  And I will set me down
My destin'd purpose to fulfil,
But with this interrupted skill
  Of thought and grief profound . . .

O thou, which on the mountain's brow,
  By night didst pray alone;
In the cold night didst pay thy vow,
And in humiliation bow,
  To thrones and pow'rs thine own.

Tell us, for thou the best can tell,
  What Melancholy means?
A guise in them that wear it well,
That goes to music to dispel
  Dark thoughts and gloomier scenes . . .

Yet thou didst preach of future bliss,
  Peace permanent above,
Of truth and mercy's holy kiss,
Those joys which none that love thee miss,
  O give us grace to love.

They are from his last book, the one which Carnan had
promised to print and sell for him: *Hymns for the Amusement
of Children*. The verse *Parables* also had been written for
children, but these are quite different. There is no sanc-
timoniousness in them and they are completely sincere.
Although writing for children, he is really speaking to himself: rebuking himself for past failures, recalling past favours,
reconciling himself to present humiliation, resigning himself
to the dreaded Debtors' Prison which he knew could not
now be avoided.

Christ Jesus, when the Twelve besought
His aid, the PATER NOSTER taught;
By giving glory we begin,
And end in deprecating sin.

Then give the glory yet again,
For who wou'd be in grief or pain,
Or brook anxiety and care,
When the quick remedy is pray'r.

Teach us in sickness to adore
Thine hand, and all our ills restore:
O let us meditate in death,
On Thee—poor man of NAZARETH.

Teach me in poverty to think
Of him who drank on Cedron's brink;
But had no mansion-house nor bread,
Or to repose him or be fed.

Teach me 'midst all the griefs below,
This transient state, this world of woe,
Submissive on my bended knee,
To take my cross and follow Thee.

Smart did not write these hymns for praise or profit, or even
to avoid prison; he wrote them to find his soul again, to re-
establish himself in childlike faith and hope and charity. By a
strange twist of fortune, it was to be his only successful book
since his confinement. It went through three editions in five
years, and only one of the perhaps numerous copies survives—in the Bodleian, from the third edition, 1775—which
probably means that they were read by many children till
they disintegrated.[1] Who knows what influence Smart may
have had on the rising generation, for example in the changing mentality towards animals:

Shall I melodious pris'ners take
From out the linnet's nest
And not keep busy care awake
To cherish ev'ry guest.

What shall I whip in cruel wrath
The steed that bears me safe,
Or 'gainst the dog, who plights his troth,
For faithful service chafe.

In the deep waters throw thy bread,
Which thou shalt find again,
With God's good interest on thy head,
And pleasure for thy pain . . .

[1] Facsimile published by Blackwell in 1947, with an introduction by
Edmund Blunden. American scholars have discovered a further printing—Philadelphia, 1791, with this addition which would have pleased
the author: "By the Rev. Christopher Smart."

187

Know when the frosty weather comes,
    'Tis charity to deal
To Wren and Redbreast all thy crumbs,
    The remnant of thy meal.

Tho' these some spirits think but light
    And deem indifferent things;
Yet they are serious in the sight
    Of CHRIST, the King of kings.

In other very simple verses Smart found his way back to
another great truth which he had somewhat lost sight of in
practice. In his longing to reach his Father's House he was
now purged of all bitterness against any human being,
however apparently hostile:

And yet I will my thoughts suppress,
    And keep my tongue from censure clear;
The Jew, the Turk, the Heathen bless,
    And hold the plough and persevere.

There's God in ev'ry man most sure,
    And ev'ry soul's to Christ allied;
If fear deject, if hopes allure,
    If Jesus wept, and pray'd and died.

To give my brother more than due,
    In talent or in name;
Nor e'en mine enemy pursue,
    To hurt or to defame.

Nay more, to bless him and to pray,
    Mine anger to controul;
And give the wages of the day
    To him that hunts my soul.

The last two lines sound as if he was already at grips with
the ghastly reality of the Debtors' Prison. "The wages of the
day" would be the pittance for the prisoner's daily food
which he might have to hand over to some bullying warder
and go hungry. One of the worst things about a Debtors'
Prison was the mental torture, which the keepers after long
practise had reduced to a fine art. The prisoner on arrival
would be flung into an unspeakably contaminated cell and
left there; on payment of a fee he would be given better
quarters; then he was told that he would be sent back to

the original cell if the fee was not raised. The screw, having been once fitted, could be tightened or relaxed as seemed most profitable.

Smart disappeared on 20 April 1770. He had been arrested and taken to the King's Bench Prison, at the bottom of the old Borough Road, Southwark, "and was there detained in the King's Prison under the custody of the Said Judges by Virtue of a Plaint Levied against him in the Said Court at the suit of James Bright in a Plea of trespass on the Case to the damage of Thirty Pounds." Lord Mansfield, who had to issue the Writ, was the man who had opened Smart's road to fame by introducing him to Pope.

On the 26th he was formally committed "for want of bail." It is not known who James Bright was; his name is not in the London directories. He had five other claims against Smart, each for the standard sum of £30. He was followed by a certain Peter Robinson on 2 May, who claimed £40 against Smart. There were probably others who would have followed him. But Robinson's claim was not proceeded with.

It was some time before Thomas Carnan discovered what had happened to his brother-in-law—how long we do not know; Hunter in his memoir merely says: "he was confined for debt in the King's Bench Prison, the rules of which he afterwards obtained by the kindness of his brother-in-law, Mr Thomas Carnan."

"The Rules" comprised a small area round the prison where debtors who could pay were allowed to circulate during the day. If a debtor could pay about ten per cent of what he was charged with, he was allowed to buy a "liberty ticket" at the cost of about four shillings a day. But that still left him with his food to buy, not to mention bribes extorted by gaolers or "garnishings" by prison gang-leaders. Carnan's money, which procured Smart the liberty of the prison, saved him from its worst physical hardships, but it probably left him to go hungry on many occasions.[1] It also left him

[1] The *Gentleman's Magazine* of July 1779 printed a note said to have been written by him to a clergyman, Rev. Mr Jackson: "Being upon the recovery from a fit of illness, and having nothing to eat, I beg you to lend me two or three shillings, which (God willing) I will return with many thanks in two or three days."

exposed to those moral evils which he probably dreaded still more.

The small area round the King's Bench was like an abscess which drew together all the evils of London without any of the healthy influences which mitigated them elsewhere. It contained 30 gin shops which sold 120 gallons weekly of this national poison (states a pamphlet of 1776), as well as floods of beer. It was a whirlpool which dragged at misery to drown itself in joyless debauchery and unfriendly lust.

A gleam of external comfort came at Christmas time when Carnan brought him the first copy of his *Hymns for Children*, published 27 December 1770. It was a little duodecimo volume, price 6d.; it did not carry his name—so as not to arouse creditors, presumably. Several of the hymns had probably been written while he was in the King's Bench that year. There is a foretaste of Blake's alarming simplicity in—

> I just came by the prison-door,
> I gave a penny to the poor:
> Papa did this good act approve,
> And poor Mamma cried out for love.

But it is not only of Blake's simplicity that these hymns are reminiscent; there is a mysterious, other-worldly allusiveness in some of them, for example in this:

> 'Tis in the spirit that attire,
>   Th' investiture of saints in heav'n,
> Those robes of intellectual fire
>   Which to the great elect are giv'n.

> 'Bring out to my returning son
>   The robes for elegance the best';
> Thus in the height it shall be done
>   And thus the penitent be blest

> 'Tis in the body, that sweet mien
>   Ingenuous Christians all possess:
> Grace, easy motions, smiles serene,
>   Clean hands and seemliness of dress.

> Whoever has thy charming pow'rs
>   Is amiable as Kidron's swan,
> Like holy Esdras feeds on flow'rs,
>   And lives on honey like St. John.

There is a Dantean quality about the hymn "Generosity" with its echoes from Virgil (I quote the first stanza only):

> That vast communicative mind,
> That form'd the world and human kind
>   And saw that all was right,
> Or was thyself, or came from Thee,
> Stupendous generosity,
>   Above all lustre bright.

At other times he remembers he is writing for children, and rhyming phrases can only partly imply the deep longing to escape from time and depend on God for all eternity:

> How brilliant past conceit each star
> Shall shine before the Lamb:
> 'Tis bliss to know not what ye are
> By knowing what I AM.

James Bright's claims against Smart were heard before a jury in February 1771. The verdict being for the plaintiff, Smart was re-committed to prison, "there to remain until he Satisfy the said James the same Damages." There was no question of his paying his debts, nor of anybody paying them for him; for, presumably, one payment would just have led to another. The verdict was in effect a death sentence. Presumably Smart was still sane and could stand on his feet when he was brought out for trial; but deterioration set in not long after.

The last news comes from Fanny Burney: not now the blushing fair of seventeen, but an old, old lady—Madame d'Arblay—looking back over the years of trying to write her father's life after she had destroyed many of his papers. Two notes from Smart's last months were preserved and quoted. One was in gratitude for money sent: "I bless God for your good nature, which please to take for a receipt." The other was to ask her father's help for a fellow-prisoner, and in it, she wrote, "he made use of an expression that pleased me much 'that he had himself assisted him, according to his willing poverty'." This is in keeping with the character given him by his nephew: "He was friendly, affectionate, and liberal to excess; so as often to give that to others of which he was in the utmost want himself."

The last recollection of Mme d'Arblay—or of her father—will not be so welcome to admirers of Smart. Looking back in sadness at the series of blows that overwhelmed him, she speaks of him ending his days in prison "under the alternate pressure of partial aberration of intellect, and bacchanalian forgetfulness of misfortune." He died—this is the correct date—on 20 May 1771, "after a short illness," adds Hunter, "of a disorder in his liver." Professors Ainsworth and Noyes suggest that the disease was cirrhosis, result of "the debilitating anodyne of strong drink." It is much more likely to have been gaol-fever in his worn-out state. In which case he would have been unable to hold solid nourishment, and alcohol would actually have prolonged his life.

He died within the rules of the King's Bench; but it is stated in the *Dictionary of National Biography*, and has been repeated by subsequent writers of his life, that his remains were buried in St Paul's Churchyard. There seems to be no way of confirming this. In the Cathedral itself there is no record of his name or of his burial. This is a little sad, for St Paul's was the mansion of his dreams in which he saw himself as "the Reviver of ADORATION amongst ENGLISH-MEN."

His dreams about a divine mission turned out to be all illusion. But in the moment that they all fell away, leaving him poor and cold and stripped of his interior comfort, it was revealed that he did have a divine message after all. His divine mission was simply to love God above all things and his neighbour as himself. It could have been a more effective love if it had not been for his mistakes and self-deception. But such as it was it persisted, pure and strong, amid the ruins of past purposes and the wrecks of human life in the Debtors' Prison.

He may have lost his reason partially towards the end; he may have got drunk sometimes when he was too ill to eat; but an epitaph can still be made up from those words which Dame Edith Sitwell wrote about him thirty years ago:

There was no room in the heaven of this madman's mind for cruelty or injustice, or for anything but love. That Heaven was undimmed by the cruelties and darkness of prison, unbroken by starvation, warm in the midst of that deathly cold. This madman of genius, this poet of genius, for all the barriers of his madness, continued to walk in the cool of the evening with his God.

Bibliography

This is not a complete bibliography. It does not include several books and articles which seemed to be sufficiently represented by quotations or summaries in later works.

A. Manuscript

The Vane Papers	by courtesy of Rt. Hon. Lord Barnard.
Cowslade MS	H. G. Archbishop King.
The Sharp Papers	Miss Lloyd-Baker and Mr. J. A. Wood.
Committee Book of St. Luke's Hospital	Dr. Richard Hunter.
Letter of Mrs. Hunter to Mrs. Smart	Reading Public Library.
Letter of Mrs. Le Noir	Bodleian 1006, f. 245.

B. Editions and Biographies of Smart

The Midwife or the Old Woman's Magazine, London, 1750–1. 2 vols.

Poems on Several Occasions, London, 1752.

A Song to David, London, 1763 (facsimile, Oxford, 1925).

Hymns for the Amusement of Children, 3rd. ed. 1775 (facsimile, Oxford, 1947).

The Poems of the late Christopher Smart (with an account of his life and writings, by his nephew Christopher Hunter), Reading, 1791, 2 vols.

A Song to David with other poems, ed. Edmund Blunden, London, 1924.

Rejoice in the Lamb, ed. William Force Stead, London, 1939.

Christopher Smart, a Biographical and Critical Study, E. G. Ainsworth and C. E. Noyes, Missouri, 1943.

The Collected Poems of Christopher Smart, ed. Norman Callan, The Muses Library, London, 1949. 2 vols.

Poems by Christopher Smart, ed. Robert Brittain, Princeton, 1950.

Jubilate Agno, ed. W. H. Bond, London, 1954.

A Song to David, ed. J. B. Broadbent, London, 1960.

Christopher Smart by Geoffrey Grigson, London, 1961.

C. Other Books

Abbey, C. J. *English Church in the Eighteenth Century*, London, 1878.

Battie, Dr. William. *Treatise on Madness*, 1758.

Burney, Frances. *Early Diary*, 1768–78, vol. I. (ed. 1889)

d'Arblay, Madame. *Memoirs of Dr. Burney*, 1832.

Burton, J. *Early Newspaper Press in Berkshire* (thesis, 1954).

Campbell, Lord. *Lives of the Lord Chancellors*, vol. V (London, 1846).

Coates. *History of Reading*, 1802.

Forster, J. *Oliver Goldsmith*, vol. I (London, ed. 1877).

George, M. *London Life in the Eighteenth Century*, London, 1925.

Toynbee and Whibley. *Thomas Gray, Correspondence*, 2 vols. (Oxford, 1935).

Holland. *Plinie's Natural History*, 1601.

Hutchinson, W. *History of Durham*, vol. III, 1794.

Hill. G. B. (ed.). *Boswell's Life of Johnson*, 6 vols. (revised edition, Oxford, 1934–40).

Hill, G. B. *Johnsonian Miscellanies*, 2 vols. (Oxford, 1897).

Jones, K. *Lunacy, Law and Conscience* (London, 1955).

Journal of the House of Commons, vol. 29 (Institute of Hist. Research).

Knight's *London*, 4 vols, 1839.

Morris, Dr. A. *The Hoxton Madhouses* (Cambridge, 1958).

Newton, D. *Catholic London* (London, 1950).

Nichols, *Literary Anecdotes of the Eighteenth Century*, 9 vols.

O'Donoghue, Rev. J. *History of Bethlehem Hospital* (London, 1911).

Overton, J. H. *William Law, Non-juror and Mystic* (London, 1881).

Quennell, P. *Hogarth's Progress* (London, 1955).

Ray. *The Wisdom of God manifested in the Works of Creation* (1691)

Surtees. *History of Durham*, vol. 4 (1840).

Sykes, N. *From Sheldon to Secker* (Cambridge, 1958).

Balderston, K. C. (ed.). *Thraliana : the Diary of Mrs Thrale, 1776–1809* (Oxford, 1951).

Welsh, C. *A Bookseller of the Last Century* (London 1885).

D. ARTICLES, EXTRACTS, ETC.

1887. Browning, R. "Parleyings with Certain People."
Seccombe, T. *Dictionary of National Biography.*

1891. Gosse, Sir E. *Gossip in a Library.*

1923. *Reading Mercury* Bicentenary Number.

1924. Falls, C. *The Critic's Armoury.*

1924. October. *Miscellanea Latomorum*, vol. IX.

1924. Murry, J. M. *Discoveries.*

1929. *The Times*, 20 May, Edmund Blunden, "A Boswellian Error."

1933. Harrison, L. *Berks. Archaeological Journal*, vol. 37.

1953. *Times Literary Supplement.* Bond, W. H. 10 April, p. 237.

1955. Sherbo, Professor A. *Notes and Queries*, February, 65–6.

1956. Sherbo, Professor A. *Modern Language Notes*, March, 172–82.

1957. Price, C. *Review of English Studies*, May, 144–8.

1959. *Notes and Queries*, November, p. 411.

1960. Merchant, Moelwyn, *Harvard Library Bulletin*, vol. XIV, No. 1.

1960. Brain, Sir Russell, in *Some Reflections on Genius*, Pitman Medical.

Index

A

ADDISON, tutor, 39, 44, 135
Aeolian lyre, 33, 34
Agricola (Aircol), 113, 124
Ainsworth, Professor, 18, 19, 71, 113, 192
Akenside, Mark, 36, 135
Allen, printer, 75
Anguish, Mr, 135, 137
Apocrypha (deutero-canonical books), 107, 108–10
"Apokatastasis", 127, 148–9
Arne, Dr, musician, 50, 129, 135

B

BATTIE, Dr William, 46, 90–101, 115, 133
Becket, St Thomas, 123
Bedlam (Bethlehem Hospital), 11, 40, 55, 81, 88–9
Berkeley, Bishop, 99
Blake, William, 190
Blunden, Edmund, 16, 20, 187
Boehme, Jacob, 169
Bond, Mr William, 20, 99, 100, 112
Boswell, James, 10, 21, 72, 80, 116, 129, 136, 153
Boulogne, 175
Boyce, organist, 50, 135, 158
Boyce, Samuel, 136
Brain, Sir Russell, 20
Brittain, Mr Robert, 19, 20, 75, 104, 172, 185
Browning, Robert, 14, 15, 139–40, 150

Burney, Charles, 40, 45, 49, 50, 116, 129, 135, 161, 182, 191–2
Burney, Fanny (Madame d'Aublay), 42, 162, 182, 185, 191–2

C

CALLAN, Professor N., 19, 42
Canonbury, house and parish, 61, 64, 72, 104, 111
Carnan, Anna-Maria (Nancy), Smart's wife, 13, 61–8, 72, 75, 82, 104, 107, 112, 113, 125–6, 135, 161, 165–6, 175–6, 180, 184
Carnan, Mary (see Hounshill)
Carnan, Thomas (her brother), 57, 62, 82, 102, 134–5, 184–6, 189
Carnan, William (her father), 13, 62
Cathars, Catharism, 122–3, 150
Chatterton, Thomas, 14
Chelsea ("Chelsey"), 116–18, 179–181
Churchill, Charles, 10, 126, 129–130, 135
Cleveland, Duchess of, 23, 29
Collins, William, 11, 14
Colman, George (the elder), 171
Cowper, William, 10, 89, 135, 168
Cowslade MS, 175
Critical Review, 132–3, 152, 154–5, 167, 185
Cruden, Alexander, 89
Cumberland, Richard, 135

D

DARLINGTON, Earl of (see Vane)

Dashwood, Sir Francis, 130
Delaval, John, Lord, 39, 43, 57,
   135, 172
Delaval, Sir Francis Blake, 43, 57,
   135, 172
Derrick, Samuel, 136
Dodsley, Robert, 36, 50, 158, 163
Dongworth, Richard, 25
Draper, Sir William, 135, 153
Dublin, 104
Durham (and Cathedral), 23, 25,
   140, 145, 149–50, 170, 171

E

ENGLAND, Church of, 15, 66–7,
   73–4, 81, 99, 107, 121–2, 126,
   130, 160–1, 168–9, 192
Esdras (Ezra), 122, 125–6

F

Fables, Smart's, 68–70
Falkiner, George, 104
Falkiner, Marianne (*see* Smart)
Falkiner, Richard, 70, 104, 135
Fielding, Henry, 10, 49, 59, 60
Fletcher, M., publisher, 138
Flexney, publisher, 129
"Franciscan", applied to Smart,
   17, 43, 151
Freemasons, 123, 141

G

GARRICK, David, 10, 57, 101–2,
   135
Gazetteer, 104, 158
Gentleman's Magazine, 57, 68, 110,
   117–18, 189
George, Saint, 113, 124
Gilpin, family, 23
Goldsmith, Oliver, 10, 46, 52, 103
Gordon, friend of Smart, 41, 135
Gosling, Francis, 94
Gray, Thomas, 10, 15, 33, 36–45,
   59, 60, 101, 135, 137
Gregory of Nyssa, 106, 127, 149
Griffiths, Ralph, 52, 103, 155
Guido (*see* Reni)

H

HAVANA, 128
Hawkesworth, Dr, 161–5
Henley, "Orator", 58–9
Hill, "Sir" John, 59, 60, 156
Hogarth, William, 10, 57, 81, 88,
   135
Hope Weir, Anne (*see* Vane)
Horace, 27, 35, 73, 163, 172–4
Hounshill, Martin, of Ringwood,
   62
Hounshill, Martin, priest, 62–3,
   82
Hounshill, Mary (Mrs Carnan,
   Mrs Newbery), 62–3, 184–5
House of Commons Inquiry,
   117–18, 130, 133
Howard, prison-reformer, 97
Hoxton, madhouses, 89, 118
Hume, David, 48
Hunter, Christopher, 13, 17, 24,
   40, 43, 47, 71, 74, 83, 96, 189,
   191–2
Hunter, Margaret (*see* Smart)
Hymn to the Supreme Being, 16,
   76–9, 85
*Hymns for the Amusement of
   Children*, 186–8, 190–1
Hymns for the Church Year, 130,
   138, 158–60

I

"ILLUMINATIVE Way", 85
"Impression", 98, 99, 174

J

JAMES, Dr, 52, 79, 104
James's Park, St, 61, 103, 114, 152,
   165, 170, 177, 181
Jeffrey, the Cat, 110, 113, 119
"Jeopardy", 80, 108, 110, 129, 131
Johnson, Samuel, 10, 21, 30, 49–
   54, 68, 71–2, 79–80, 82, 89, 104,
   116, 129, 135–6
Jubilate Agno, 17, 21, 28–9, 34,
   67, 79–80, 84, 87, 96, 98–100,
   105–15, 118–27, 130, 141, 145–8,
   174, 180–1

K

KEATS, 14, 15
Keith, "Bishop", 66
Kempe, John, 185
Kenrick, William, 57, 59, 71, 135, 153
Kent, 23, 24
King, Keeper of Turlington House, 117, 133

L

LAW, William, 73, 142, 169
Leach, Dryden, Printer, 158, 169, 184
Le Noir, Mrs (see Smart)
Leo, Pope Saint, 159
Lincoln's Inn Fields Chapel, 63
Livermore (Levermore), Ezra, 94
Locke, John, 97, 98
Lowth, Dr, 99, 164, 168
Luke's Hospital, St, 88–97, 101

M

MAIDSTONE, 25
Maloney, J. B., priest, 82
Mansfield (see Murray)
Mapledurham, 62
Martial Review, 103
Marvell, Andrew, 25, 32, 38, 89
Mary, Blessed Virgin, 74, 142, 147, 157
Mason, William, 59, 101, 135, 137, 171, 177, 184
Merrick, James, 134, 165, 167–8
Midwife, The, 53–9
Miles's Madhouse, 118, 133
Milton, John, 15, 38
"Moabites", 67, 113, 121, 125, 161
Monro, Dr, 91, 133
Monthly Review, 13, 14, 52, 152, 155–6, 158, 167, 174
Moorfields, Chapel, 63, 67, 82
More, Henry, 31
Morris, Dr Arthur, 89
Munificence and Modesty, 155–7
Murphy, Arthur, 50, 54, 59, 60, 102, 135

Murray, William, Lord Mansfield, 30, 129, 133, 189
Murry, Middleton, 16
Museum, 47, 82

N

NARES, musician, 158, 164
Newbery, family, 62–3
Newbery, John, 51, 52, 61–4, 66, 73, 75, 82, 94, 102, 103, 134–5, 163, 165, 175
Newbury, Mrs (see Hounshill)
Nichol's, *Literary Anecdotes*, 91
North Briton, 130, 145
Northington, Lord Chancellor, 11, 81
Noyes, Professor, 18, 19, 71, 113, 192

O

ODE to St Cecilia, Smart's, 36, 38, 46, 51
On a Bed of Guernsey Lilies, 131, 157–8, 183
Origen, 127
Oxford and Cambridge Miscellany, 52–3

P

"PANTOKRATOR", 149
Panton, Paul, 170–2, 177, 179
Paul's, St, Church, 169, 192
Piozzi (see Thrale)
Plato, Platonism, 11, 24, 31, 98
Pliny's *Natural History*, 109
Pocock, Admiral, 128, 153
Pope, Alexander, 9, 29, 30, 36, 38, 59
Powell, Rev. Mr, 135
Pratt, Harriot, 36, 41, 42, 47, 63
Pratt, Jermyn, 36, 41, 135
Psalms, Smart's translation of, 13, 130, 134, 137, 138, 142–3, 158, 169
Public Advertiser, 101–2
"Purgative Way", 84

R

RABY Castle, 25, 26, 28, 178

Rambler, The, 49, 54

Randall, friend of Smart, 41, 135, 158

Reading, *Reading Mercury,* 13, 16, 62, 68, 165, 175

Reason and Imagination, 135, 153–4

Reni, Guido, 157

Richardson, Samuel, 59

Rolt, Richard, 50, 54, 75, 102–3, 132

Rome, Church of, 63, 66–7, 82, 107, 114, 121, 126, 160–1, 169, 175–6

Roubiliac (Roubillac), 59, 125

Ruth, 67, 113

S

SAY, Charles, printer, 158

Seatonian Prize Poems, 9, 12, 50–1, 58–9, 70, 73

Seven Years War, 67, 103, 121

Sharp, Archdeacon, 169–70

Sharp, Granville, 170, 182

Sheeles, Miss, A. F., 132, 135, 157

Sheeles, Rev. James, 129, 132, 135

Sherbo, Professor, 21, 110, 128

Sherratt, John, 131–2, 135, 153, 157

Sitwell, Dame Edith, 16, 119, 192–193

Smart, ancestors, of Snotterton, 23

Smart, Elizabeth (Mrs Le Noir), Chr's daughter, 14, 24, 26, 64, 65, 66, 72, 111, 125, 168, 175–6

Smart, Francis, of Snotterton, Chr's cousin, 23, 25, 111–12, 137, 175, 177–80

Smart, John, of Snotterton, Chr's uncle, 23, 25, 178

Smart, Margaret (Mrs Hunter), Chr's sister, 23, 24, 26, 70, 135, 161, 163–6

Smart, Marianne (Mrs Falkiner), Chr's sister, 23, 70, 104, 135

Smart, Marianne (Polly), Chr's elder daughter, 64, 65, 66, 67, 111, 125, 175–6

Smart, Peter, Chr's father, 23, 25

Smart, Richard, attorney, 111–12, 137, 177–80

Smart, Winifred (*née* Griffiths), Chr's mother, 23, 25, 111–12, 161, 163–6, 180

Smollett, 10, 135, 152

Snotterton, 23, 111, 175, 178–9

Song to David, A, 9, 13, 14, 15, 22, 34, 51, 73, 120, 127, 137–53, 158, 174

Southwell, Robert, 77

Spenser, Edmund, 29, 76–7

Staindrop, 22, 28, 29, 112, 178

Stead, W. F., 17, 93, 121, 128

Stonhewer, friend of Smart, 41, 135, 137, 171, 184

Stuart, House of, 35, 123

Surtees, Historian of Durham, 65–66

T

THOMSON, James, 11

Thornton, Bonnell, 53, 54

Thrale, Mrs, 72, 80, 83, 99, 116, 119, 129, 181

Turlington, Robert (his "House"), 117–9, 129 133–4

Tyers, Thomas, 30, 50, 129, 136

Tyler, Rev. Mr, 135

U

"UNITIVE Way", 86

Universal Visitor, 75, 79

Ursulines, 66, 175

V

VANE, Anne (Lady Anne Hope Weir), 26, 27, 28

Vane, Christopher, first Lord Barnard, 23

Vane, Henry, third Lord Barnard, first Earl of Darlington, 25, 26, 28, 73–5, 135

Vane, Henry, fourth Lord Barnard, second Earl of Darlington, 26, 135, 178–9

Vauxhall Gardens, 50, 53, 57

Voltaire, 59, 101
Vows, 113–14, 120–1, 172, 181

W

WALPOLE, Horace, 37, 66
Waltham, St Lawrence, 62
Warburton, Bishop, 73, 106, 168
Warton (Wharton), Joseph, 11, 135
Warton (Wharton), Thomas, 11, 37, 39, 45, 135

Webster, Dr, 106
Wesley, John, 11, 81, 97, 107, 168
Whitfield, George, 11, 81
Wilkes, John, 130, 135, 152
Williamson, H. Ross, 123
Wordsworth, 14, 157
Worgan, 57, 157
Woty, 103, 135
Wright's Madhouse, 89